When Someone Dies
IN ARIZONA

ALL THE LEGAL AND PRACTICAL THINGS
YOU NEED TO DO
WHEN SOMEONE NEAR TO YOU DIES
IN THE STATE OF ARIZONA

By AMELIA E. POHL, Attorney at Law
with PAUL B. BARTLETT
as consulting Arizona attorney
and
BARBARA J. SIMMONDS, Ph.D.
as consulting psychologist

 EAGLE PUBLISHING COMPANY OF BOCA

EAGLE PUBLISHING COMPANY OF BOCA
4199 N. Dixie Highway, #2
Boca Raton, FL   33431
E-mail   eagleonline@ibm.net

WEB SITE   http://www.eaglepublishing.com
Telephone orders: 1-800-824-0823
or fax orders to: 561-338-0823

Printed in the United States of America
ISBN 1-892407-04-3

Library of Congress Catalog Card Number: 99-73880

About the Author

Before becoming an attorney in 1985, AMELIA E. POHL taught mathematics on both the high school and college level. During her tenure as Associate Professor of Mathematics at Prince George's Community College in Maryland, she wrote several books including Probability: A Set Theory Approach, Principals of Counting and Common Stock Sense.

During her practice of law Attorney Pohl observed that many people want to reduce the high cost of legal fees by performing or assisting with their own legal transactions. Attorney Pohl found that, with a bit of guidance, people are able to perform many legal transactions for themselves. Attorney Pohl is utilizing her background as teacher, author and attorney to provide that "bit of guidance" to the general public in the form of self-help legal books that she has written. Attorney Pohl is currently working on "translating" this book for the rest of the 49 states:

When Someone Dies In Arkansas
When Someone Dies in Alaska, etc.

Consulting Psychologist

BARBARA J. SIMMONDS, Ph.D., a noted psychologist, has collaborated with the author on those sections of this book dealing with the grieving process. Dr. Simmonds has been practicing in the field of Health/Rehabilitation Psychology and Gerontology for the past 10 years. As a natural outcome, her experiences in the field led her to develop expertise in Grief Counseling.

In addition to her work in hospitals, nursing centers and private practice, Dr. Simmonds has served as Adjunct Faculty at Nova Southeastern University, teaching courses in Aging, Stress Management and Grief Counseling. Dr. Simmonds holds a Master's Degree in Gerontology and a Ph.D. in Clinical Psychology from Nova Southeastern University. She was the Director of Psychological Services at Villa Maria Nursing and Rehabilitation Center for eight years and now continues her relationship with the institution on a consultation basis. She continues with her private practice in North Miami, Florida.

Consulting Arizona Attorney

PAUL B. BARTLETT, ESQ. has been a member of the Arizona State Bar since 1976. He received his Bachelor of Arts degree with honors from the University of Wisconsin, Madison in 1972. He earned his Juris Doctor from Syracuse College of Law in 1975. Paul Bartlett has been practicing in Tucson since 1976. He concentrates in the field of Elder Law (Trusts, Estates, Probate, Medicaid Planning, Guardianship and Conservatorships). In 1983, while teaching an evening Hebrew course, two students came to class dejected. They had been informed that five of their relatives were diagnosed with Alzheimers's disease within the space of one month. The students subsequently formed a local chapter of the Alzheimer's Association and prevailed on Paul to volunteer his services. He soon found himself elected as President of the chapter. Today he remains as an active Board member. Paul also has served as President of the Arizona State Chapter of the National Academy of Elderlaw Attorneys. Paul volunteers as a Pima County Superior Court Judge Pro Tem. When he is not practicing law, Paul swims on a Masters Swim Team, concertizes with the guitar and sings in Hebrew, Arabic, Spanish and Ladino.

Paul B. Bartlett has a web site at www.tucsonelderlaw.com.

To my brother, Paul Adinolfi,
his intelligence, good humor and kindness,
his strength during our times of family loss,
have set the beacon standard for me to follow.

ACKNOWLEDGEMENT

When someone dies, the family attorney is often among the first to be called. Family members have questions about whether probate is necessary, who to notify, how to get possession of the assets, etc.

Over the years, as I practiced in the field of Elder Law, I noticed that the questions raised were much the same family to family. It occurred to me that a book answering such questions might be of service to the general public; so I wish to thank all of the clients whom I have had the honor and pleasure to serve, for providing me with the impetus to write this book.

In addition, I wish to express my sincere appreciation for the assistance and encouragement given to me by Margot Bosche, Louise Lucas, RN, Paul R. Federico, Michael J. DeMarie, CPA, Ann Apicella Grodzicki, Mary Richards, Ph.D., Martha Dermer, and my husband, J. William Pohl. Their insightful suggestions were invaluable.

When Someone Dies in Arizona

CONTENTS

About this book

The author has tried to make this book as comprehensive as possible so there are specialized sections of the book that do not apply to the general population and may not be of interest to you. The following GUIDE POSTS appear throughout the book. You can read the section if the situation applies to you or skip the section if it doesn't.

GUIDE POSTS

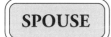

The SPOUSE POST means that the information provided is specifically for the spouse of the decedent. If the decedent was single, then skip this section.

The COMPUTER POST means that additional information is available on the Internet. The COMPUTER POST is followed by an Internet address of a web site where you can obtain the information. If you are not a computer buff, then you can skip this section.

The CALL-A-LAWYER POST alerts you to a situation that may require the assistance of an attorney.

 The SPECIAL SITUATION POST means that the information given in that paragraph applies to a particular event or situation; for example, when the decedent dies a violent death. If the situation does not apply in your case then you can skip the section.

 The CAUTION POST alerts you to a potential problem. It is followed by a suggestion about how to avoid the problem.

GLOSSARY

This book is designed for the average reader. Legal terminology has been kept to a minimum. There is a glossary at the end of the book in the event you come across a legal term that is not familiar to you.

STATE AND FEDERAL STATUTES

Where applicable, we have identified the Arizona or federal statute that is the basis of the discussion. For example, the notation (AZ 11-597) refers to section 597 of Title 11 of the Arizona Revised Statutes. If you wish to read the statute as it is written, then you can look it up in the statute section located at your local courthouse library, as well as in most public libraries.

 You can find the complete set of Arizona statutes at: http://www.azleg.state.az.us and the set of federal statutes at http://www4.law.cornell.edu/uscode

FICTITIOUS NAMES AND EVENTS

The examples in this book are based loosely on actual events; however, all names are fictitious and the events, as portrayed, are fictitious.

HOW TO FIND A LAWYER

This book explains what needs to be done to settle the affairs of the decedent, but laws change frequently and you should to seek the counsel of an attorney if you have any legal question. When looking for an attorney, consider three things: EXPERTISE, COST and PERSONALITY.

EXPERTISE

The State Bar of Arizona has certification programs for eight areas of practice: Bankruptcy, Criminal, Estate & Trust, Family Law, Injury & Wrongful Death, Real Estate, Tax and Worker's Compensation. Those certified in Estate & Trust are experienced in Probate matters. To be certified as a specialist in a certain type of law the attorney must have practiced a number of years in that type of law (usually 5) and must pass an Arizona Bar certification examination. You can call the State Bar of Arizona at (602) 340-7300 and they will provide you with a list of attorneys who are specialists in each of these areas.

Certification is just one of the criteria to consider. Many fine attorneys are experienced in an area of law, but have not taken the time, effort and expense to become certified. If the attorney is not a specialist in the branch of law that you need, then ask how long he has practiced that type of law and what percentage of his practice is devoted to that type of law. Of course the best way to find an attorney, experienced in the type of law you seek, is through personal referral. Ask your friends, family or business acquaintances if they have used an attorney for the field of law that you seek and whether they were pleased with the results.

The Arizona Bar web site contains a list of Lawyer Referal Services throughout the state. Their MEMBER FINDER section lists the name, address, phone number and area of practice for each Arizona attorney.

 STATE BAR OF ARIZONA WEB SITE
http://www.azbar.org/FindingLawyer

COST
In addition to the attorney's experience, it is important that you check out what you can expect to pay in attorney's fees. When you call for an appointment ask what the attorney will charge for the initial consultation and the approximate cost for the service you seek. Ask whether there will be any additional costs such as filing fees, accounting fees, expert witness fees, etc.

If the least expensive attorney is out of your price range then there are two state agencies that provide legal assistance. The ARIZONA MODEST MEANS PROJECT offers legal assistance for those who cannot afford an attorney, but who make too much money to qualify for free legal services. They provide a free 30 minute initial consultation and an hourly rate thereafter of $30 per hour. You reach them at (602) 266-2322.

For other agencies that offer counseling to persons with low income, you can look in the telephone book for the Legal Aid or Legal Service office nearest you or you can call (602) 252-4804 and they will refer you the office nearest you.

PERSONALITY

Of equal importance to the attorney's experience and legal fees, is your relationship with the attorney. How easy was it to reach the attorney? Did you go through layers of receptionists and legal assistants before being allowed to speak to the attorney? Did the attorney promptly return your call? If you had difficulty reaching the attorney, then you can expect similar problems should you employ that attorney.

Did the attorney treat you with respect? Did the attorney treat you paternally with a "father knows best" attitude or did the attorney treat you as an intelligent person with the ability to understand the options available to you and the ability to make your own decision based on the information provided to you?

Are you able to understand and easily communicate with the attorney? Is he/she speaking to you in plain English or is his/her explanation of the matter so full of legalese to be almost meaningless to you?

Do you find the attorney's personality to be pleasant or grating? Sometimes people rub each other the wrong way. It is like rubbing a cat the wrong way. Stroking a cat from head to tail is pleasing to the cat, but petting it in the opposite direction, no matter how well intended, causes friction. If the lawyer makes you feel annoyed or uncomfortable, then find another attorney.

It is worth the effort to take the time to interview as many attorneys as it takes to find one with the right expertise, fee schedule and personality for you.

CHAPTER 1
THE FIRST WEEK

Dealing with the death of a close family member or friend is difficult. Not only do you need to deal with your own emotions but often with those of your family and friends. Sometimes their sorrow is more painful to you, than what you are experiencing yourself.

In addition to the emotional impact of a death, there are many things that need to be done, from arranging the funeral and burial, to closing out the business affairs of the decedent, and finally giving whatever property is left to the proper beneficiary.

The funeral and burial take only a few days. Wrapping up the affairs of the decedent may take considerably longer. This chapter explains what things you (the spouse or closest family member) need to do during the first week, beginning at the moment of death and continuing through the funeral.

 MALE GENDER USED

Rather than use "he/she" or "his/her" for simplicity
(and hoping not to offend anyone)
we will refer to the decedent using the male gender.

References to other people will be in both genders.

AUTOPSIES

Years ago people died natural deaths from unknown causes. Doctors often requested permission to perform an autopsy to determine the cause of death. In today's high tech world of medicine, doctors are fairly certain of the cause of death, but if there is a question, the family may be asked permission to perform an autopsy.

If, during his lifetime, the decedent signed a Medical Power of Attorney or a Living Will in which he either authorized an autopsy, or appointed a *health care surrogate* (someone to make his medical decisions) and gave the surrogate the right to authorize an autopsy, then the surrogate can agree, in writing, to the autopsy. If such is not the case, then whomever assumes responsibility for the burial, has the right to agree to the autopsy, in the following order:

1. Father   2. Mother   3. Husband   4. Wife
5. Adult Child   6. Guardian   7. Next of Kin

If none of these are available, then a friend or anyone who has the responsibility of the burial can authorize the autopsy (AZ 36-832).

The cost of an autopsy runs anywhere from $2,500 to $3,500. The person giving authorization must agree to pay for the autopsy because the cost is not covered under most health insurance plans. It is in the family's best interest to consent to the autopsy because such examination might reveal a genetic disorder, that could be treated if it later appears in another family member.

An example that comes to mind is a woman who was taken to the hospital complaining of stomach pains. The doctors diagnosed her as suffering from gallbladder disease but she died before they could effectively treat her. A doctor suggested that an autopsy be performed to determine the actual cause of death.

The woman had three daughters, one of whom objected to the autopsy: "Why spend that kind of money?
It won't bring Mom back."

The daughter's wishes were respected, however over the years the daughters aged and became ill with her own various ailments they would undergo physical examinations. As part of taking their medical history, doctors would routinely ask "And what was cause of your mother's death?" None could answer the question.

This is not a dramatic story. No mysterious genetic disorder ever occurred in any daughter, nor in any of their children. But each daughter (including the one who objected) at some point in their life, was confronted with the nagging question "What did Mom die of?"

MANDATORY AUTOPSIES

When a person dies, a physician must sign the death certificate stating the cause of death. If a person dies in a hospital, then there is a doctor present to sign the certificate. If a person dies at home from natural causes or any other reason (accident, violence, suicide) then the police must be notified. The person who discovers the body should call 911 to summon the police.

The police will investigate the matter and ask the Medical Examiner to determine the cause of death. If there is a suspicion that the death was not from natural causes or if the decedent died from a disease that might pose a threat to the public health, then the Medical Examiner will consult with the county attorney or the Superior court judge in the county where the decedent died to determine whether an autopsy should be conducted (AZ 11-597 (A)).

AUTOPSIES PERFORMED BY THE INSURANCE COMPANY

Most accident and life insurance policies contain a provision that the company has the right to perform an autopsy. The cost of the autopsy is paid for by the insurance company, so they will not order an autopsy unless there is some important reason to do so.

ANATOMICAL GIFTS

If, before death, the decedent made an anatomical gift by signing a donor card then hospital personnel or the donor's doctor needs to be made aware of the gift in quick proximity to the time of death — preferably before death.

GIFT AUTHORIZED BY THE FAMILY

Hospital personnel determine whether a mortally ill patient is a candidate for an organ donation. Early on in the donor program those over 65 were not considered as suitable candidates. Today, however, the condition of the organ, and not the age, is the determining factor.

The federal government has established regional Organ Procurement Organizations throughout the United States, based on area population, to coordinate the donor program. The Organ Procurement Organization for the state of Arizona is located in Phoenix. It is called the DONOR NETWORK OF ARIZONA. If it is decided that the patient is a candidate, the hospital will contact the Donor Network who will determine whether the patient is a suitable donor. If they decide to request the gift and the candidate did not sign a donor card then someone in the family must give written permission. Someone who is specially trained will approach the family to request the donation. Arizona statute 36-843 establishes an order of priority to authorize the donation:

1st   The agent appointed in the decedent's
        health care power of attorney
2nd The decedent's court appointed guardian (if any)
3rd   The spouse, unless legally separated
4th   A majority of the decedent's adult children
5th   A parent of the decedent
6th   If unmarried, the decedent's adult partner, if no
        one else has assumed financial responsibility
7th   A close friend of the decedent

If permission is obtained from a family member and there are others in the same or a higher priority, then an effort must be made to contact those people and ask their permission. For example, if the brother of the decedent agrees to the gift (7th in priority) and the decedent had adult children who are reasonably available for consultation (5th in priority) then the children need to be made aware of the gift. No gift can be made unless a majority of the children agree to the gift. Similarly, the statute prohibits the gift if the decedent ever expressed his opposition to a donation.

AFTER THE DONATION

If the DONOR NETWORK OF ARIZONA and the family agree to the donation, then once the operation is complete the body is delivered to the funeral home and prepared for burial or cremation as directed by the family. The operation does not disfigure the body so there can be an open casket viewing if the family so wishes.

Once the donation is made, the Donor Network keeps in touch with the donor's family. They will provide the family with basic demographic information about the donation, such as the age, sex, marital status, number of children and occupation of the recipient of the gift. If the donor's family wishes, the Donor Network will provide them with updates during the year following the donation.

If the recipient of the gift wishes to write to the donor's family to thank them for the gift, the Donor Network will contact the donor's family and ask if they wish to receive the letter. If not, then the letter is kept on file in the event that the donor's family may want to read it at a later date.

GIFT FOR EDUCATION OR RESEARCH

If the decedent signed a donor card indicating his wish to use his body for any purpose and he is not a candidate for an organ donation, then you can offer to release the body to the University of Arizona, Department of Cell Biology and Anatomy to be used for education or research:

University of Arizona
College of Medicine
Department of Cell Biology and Anatomy
1501 North Campbell Avenue
Tucson, AZ 85724-5044

You will need to call the University at (520) 626-1801 within 24 hours after the death to determine whether they will accept the body. The University will not accept bodies from those who have died from a contagious disease or from crushing injuries or who are extremely obese. If they accept the donation, they will charge a mortuary service fee that can range anywhere from $65 to $425.

It takes about 18 months to complete an educational or scientific project. Once the project is complete the remains are cremated and ashes returned to the family.

THE FUNERAL

Approximately one third of the population dies suddenly from an accident or undetected illness. Two thirds of the population die after being ill for a year or more with the most common scenario being that of an aged person dying after being ill for several months. In such cases, the death is expected. Family and friends are emotionally prepared for the happening. Whether expected or unexpected, the first job is the disposition of the body.

THE PRE-ARRANGED FUNERAL

Increasingly, people are making advance arrangements for their own funeral and burial. This makes it easier on the family both financially and emotionally. All decisions have been made and there is no guessing what the decedent would have wanted.

If the decedent made provision for his burial space, then you need to locate the burial certificate. If the decedent purchased a pre-need funeral plan, then you need to locate the contract. You should read the contract to determine what provisions were made. Some contracts are paid on an installment basis. If the decedent signed such a contract, then you need to find out what monies were paid and whether there is a remaining balance due.

If you cannot locate the contract, but you know the name of the funeral home, then call and ask them to send you a copy of the contract. If you believe the decedent purchased a funeral plan but you do not know the name of the funeral home, then call all of the local funeral homes. Many local funeral homes are part of a national funeral company with computer capacity to identify people who have purchased a contract in any of their many locations.

Once you have possession of the contract, bring it with you to the funeral home and go over the terms of the contract with the funeral director. Inquire whether there is any charge that is not included in the contract.

MAKING FUNERAL ARRANGEMENTS

If the decedent died unexpectedly or without having made any prior funeral arrangements then your first job is to choose a funeral director and make arrangements for the funeral or cremation. Most people choose the nearest or most conveniently located funeral home without comparison shopping; however prices for these services can vary significantly from funeral home to funeral home. Savings can be had if you take the time to make a few phone calls.

Receiving price quotes by telephone is your right under Arizona law. Arizona statute 32-1375 requires a funeral director to give accurate telephone quotes of the retail prices of his goods and services. Funeral homes are listed in the telephone directory under FUNERAL DIRECTORS. If you live in a small town, there may be only one or two listings. If such is the case, then check out some funeral homes in the next largest city.

Funeral Directors usually provide the following services:
➢ arrange for the transportation of the body to the funeral home and then to the burial site
➢ obtain burial transit permits
➢ arrange for the embalming or cremation of the body
➢ arrange funeral and memorial services and the viewing of the body
➢ obtain information for the death certificate
➢ order copies of the death certificate for the family
➢ have memorial cards printed

To compare prices you will need to determine:
✧ what is included in the price of a basic funeral plan
✧ whether you can expect any additional cost.

Embalming is necessary if you are going to have a viewing. Embalming is not necessary if you order a direct cremation or an immediate burial. Federal Trade Commission Rule 453.5 prohibits the funeral home from charging an embalming fee unless you order the service.

If the decedent did not own a burial space, then that cost must be included when making funeral arrangements.

PURCHASING THE CASKET

When comparison-shopping, you will find that the single most expensive item in the funeral arrangement is the casket. Most funeral directors will quote you a price for the basic funeral plan. That plan does not include the cost of the casket. Directors usually quote a range of prices for the casket, saying that you will need to come in and choose the casket at the time you contract for the funeral.

When selecting a casket you should be aware that there is often a considerable mark-up in the price quoted by the funeral director. You do not need to deal "sole source" in the purchase of the casket. You can purchase a casket elsewhere and have it delivered to the funeral home for use instead of the one offered by the funeral director.

In 1994, The Federal Trade Commission ruled that funeral homes had to accept caskets purchased elsewhere. (FTC Rule 453.4). The ruling includes a ban on funeral homes charging a handling fee for accepting a casket purchased elsewhere.

If you wish to shop for a casket, then the best time to do so is before you go to the funeral home to arrange for the funeral. You can find a retail casket sales outlet in the telephone book under CASKETS. You may need to look in the telephone directory for the nearest large city to find a listing. For users of the Internet, you can use your search engine to find the retail sales casket company nearest you. By making a call to a retail casket sales dealer, you will become knowledgeable in the price range of caskets. You can then decide what is a reasonable price for the product you seek.

Once you have determined what you should pay for the casket, it is only fair to give the funeral director the opportunity to meet that price. If you cannot reach a meeting of the minds, then you can always order the casket from the retail sales dealer and have it delivered to the funeral home.

THE CREMATION

Increasingly people are opting for cremation. The reasons for choosing cremation are varied, but for the majority, it is a matter of finances. The cost of cremation is approximately one-sixth that of an ordinary funeral and burial. A major saving is the cost of the casket. No casket is necessary for the cremation. Both Federal law and Arizona state law prohibit a Funeral Director from requiring that you buy a casket when the body is being cremated. Of course, if you want to have a viewing of the body and/or a funeral service with the body present, then you will need to rent a casket from the Funeral Director for the service.

If you are having a memorial service in a place of worship with no viewing of the body before the cremation, then consider contracting with a facility that does cremations only. Look in the telephone book CREMATION SERVICES. These facilities provide much the same services as a funeral home but with one important exception — the Cremation Service does not provide any type of funeral service or public viewing of the body.

 THE OVERWEIGHT DECEDENT

If the decedent weighs more than 300 pounds, then you need to check to see if the Cremation service has facilities large enough to handle the body. If you cannot locate a crematory that can accommodate the body, then you will need to make burial arrangements.

DISPOSING OF THE ASHES

The decedent's ashes can be buried in a cemetery or in a mausoleum or scattered in a large body of water. If the ashes are to be buried, you will need to obtain a suitable urn for the burial. You can purchase the urn from the Funeral Director or Crematory Service Director. Urns cost much less than caskets, but they can cost several hundred dollars. You may wish to do some comparison shopping by calling a retail sales casket dealer.

 BURYING THE INDIGENT

There are no state owned or maintained cemeteries in the State of Arizona. Each county decides how to dispose of the remains of the indigent or unidentified decedent. If a person dies of natural causes and the identity of the person cannot be determined, the Medical Examiner in the county in which the body was found will have the body delivered to a local funeral establishment. They will perform the normal county indigent burial, in the manner and for the fee then being paid by the county. (AZ 11-600)

If an indigent person dies and the police can determine his identity, they will try to locate the family. If the decedent was an honorably discharged veteran, then the Veteran's Administration will arrange for a burial. If the decedent was not an honorably discharged veteran and his family is unable or unwilling to make burial arrangements, the Medical Examiner will arrange for an indigent county burial.

> **Special
> Situation**

THE VIOLENT DEATH

If the decedent died a violent death or under circumstances in which foul play is suspected, the Medical Examiner will take possession of the body. The body will not be released to the funeral director until the examination of the body is complete. In the interim, the family can proceed with arrangements for the funeral. The funeral director will contact the Medical Examiner to determine when he can pick up the body and proceed with the funeral

 **☎ LAWYER** | ACCIDENTAL OR CRIMINAL DEATH

If the decedent died because of an accident then it is important to contact a Personal Injury attorney to determine whether the family has a case for wrongful death. If the accident was related to the decedent's job, the family may wish to consult with a Worker's Compensation attorney as well.

If the decedent died because of a criminal act and you are a family member, then you may wish to contact an attorney experienced in Criminal Law to learn of your rights as a member of the family

THE MISSING PERSON

If a person is missing for 5 years, and his absence is unexplained, even after a thorough search has been conducted, then that person is presumed to be dead (AZ 12-509). It is important to consult with an attorney to determine how to establish the date of disappearance, and then to have the person declared dead, so that a probate procedure can begin after the 5 year period.

| Special Situation | THE OUT OF STATE BURIAL |

If the decedent is to be buried in another state, then the body will need to be transported to that state. Most funeral homes belong to a national network of funeral homes, and the out-of-state Funeral Director has the means to make local arrangements to ship the body. You can contact the out-of-state Funeral Director and have him/her make arrangement with the airline for the transportation of the body.

If services are to be held in Arizona and in another state, then you can contact you local funeral director home and he will make arrangements with the out-of-state funeral home to transport the body.

If the body has been cremated, then you can transport the ashes yourself, either by carrying the ashes as part of your luggage or by arranging with the airline to transport the ashes as cargo. You should have a certified copy of the death certificate available in the event that you need to identify the remains of the decedent. Call the airline before departure and ask whether they have any special regulation or procedure regarding the transportation of human ashes.

THE MILITARY BURIAL

Subject to availability of burial spaces, an honorably discharged veteran and/or his unmarried minor or handicapped child and/or his un-remarried spouse may be buried in a national military cemetery. Some cemeteries have room only for cremated remains or for the casketed remains of a family member of someone who is currently buried in that cemetery, so you need to call for space availability.

There are two national military cemeteries in Arizona:
NATIONAL MEMORIAL CEMETERY OF ARIZONA
23029 North Cave Creek Road
Phoenix, AZ 85024

PRESCOTT NATIONAL CEMETERY
VA Medical Center
500 Highway 89 North
Prescott, AZ 86301

For information about burials at either of these cemeteries call (602) 379-4615.

The Department of the Army is in charge of the Arlington National Cemetery. If you wish to have an eligible deceased veteran buried in the Arlington National Cemetery, then call them at (703) 695-3250.
Arlington National Cemetery
Interment Service Branch
Arlington, VA 22211

THE COST OF A MILITARY BURIAL

Burial space in a National Cemetery is free of charge. Cemetery employees will open and close the grave and mark it with headstone or grave marker without cost to the family. The local Veteran's Administration ("VA") will provide the family with a memorial flag.

If the decedent was receiving a VA pension then the VA will pay a burial and funeral expense allowance regardless of where the veteran is buried. The VA will not reimburse any burial or funeral cost for the spouse of a veteran.

For information about reimbursement of funeral and burial expenses you can call the VA at 1-800-827-1000.

VA WEB SITE

The Department of Veteran's Affairs has a web site
http://www.cem.va.gov

The site has information about the following topics
> National and Military Cemeteries
> Burial, Headstones and Markers
> State Cemetery Grants Program
> Obtaining Military Records
> Locating Veterans

SPOUSE

BENEFITS FOR SPOUSE OF DECEDENT VETERAN

If the decedent was honorably discharged, then regardless of where he is buried, his spouse might be eligible for a contribution from the Veteran's Administration for his funeral and burial expenses. If the decedent had minor or disabled children, his spouse may also be eligible for a monthly benefit of Dependency and Indemnity Compensation ("DIC").

If the Veteran's surviving spouse receives nursing home care under Medicaid, then the spouse might be eligible for a $90 monthly payment from the VA.

Whether a surviving spouse is eligible for any of these benefits depends on many factors including whether the decedent served on active duty, the cause of his death, and the surviving spouse's assets and income.

For information about whether the surviving spouse is eligible for any benefit related to the decedent's military service call the VETERANS ADMINISTRATION at 1-800-827-1000.

You can receive a printed statement of public policy by requesting VA Pamphlet 051-000-00217-2 entitled FEDERAL BENEFITS FOR VETERANS AND DEPENDENTS. Send a check in the amount of $5 to:

THE SUPERINTENDENT OF DOCUMENTS
P.O. Box 371954
Pittsburgh, PA 15250-7954

If your wish to pay by VISA or Master Card you can order by telephone 1-202-512-1800 or by FAX to 1-202-512-2250

THE OFFENSIVE FUNERAL OR BURIAL

The funeral and burial industry is well regulated by the state and federal government. Under Arizona statue 32-1301(54) the following acts are subject to disciplinary action:

- ⊠ Delivering goods of a lesser quality than that presented to the purchaser as a sample
- ⊠ Using a false or misleading advertisement
- ⊠ Paying kick-backs to generate business

Funeral directors are licensed professionals so it is unusual to have a problem with the funeral or burial or cremation. If, however, you had a bad experience with any aspect of the funeral then you can file a complaint with the state licensing agency:

State Board of Funeral Directors and Embalmers
1400 W. Washington, Room 230
Phoenix, AZ   85007
(602) 542-3095

This agency does not license cemeteries, so if your complaint has to do with the burial you can contact the state consumer protection agency of the Office of the Attorney General at (602) 542-3702 or you can call their toll free number (800) 352-8431.

If you are not satisfied with the results obtained, then consult with an attorney who is experienced in litigation matters.

THE DEATH CERTIFICATE

The Funeral Director or Cremation Service Director will order as many death certificates as you request. Most establishments require an original certified copy and not a photocopy so you need to order sufficient certified copies.

The following is a list of institutions that may want a certified copy:

❋ Each insurance company that insured the decedent or his property (health insurance company, life insurance company, car insurance company, home insurance company)

❋ Each financial institution in which the decedent had money invested (brokerage houses, banks)

❋ The decedent's pension fund

❋ Each credit card company used by the decedent

❋ The IRS

❋ The Social Security Administration

❋ The County Recorder in each county where the decedent owned real property.

Some airlines and car rental companies offer a discount for short notice, emergency trips. If you have family flying in for the funeral, you may wish to order a few extra copies of the death certificate so that they can obtain an airline or car rental discount.

ORDERING COPIES OF THE DEATH CERTIFICATE

If you wish to order certified copies of the death certificate at a later date, you can call the funeral director and ask him to do so or you can write to:

Arizona Department of Health Services
Vital Records Section
P.O. Box 3887
Phoenix, AZ   85030

or you can apply in person for the death certificate at:

Arizona Department Of Health Services
Vital Records Section
2727 W. Glendale Avenue
Phoenix, AZ   85051

You may save some time by first calling **The Office of Vital Records (602) 255-3260** and asking what information they require.   The Office will issue death certificates only to the immediate family, or the funeral director or attorney on behalf of a member of the immediate family. The Office of Vital Records requires that you have your request notarized, or that you submit a picture identification of yourself, such as a copy of your driver's license.

The present charge is $6 for each certified copy. They accept personal checks made payable to the Office of Vital Records; however, they will not send the certificate until the check clears. To avoid delay you may wish to pay with a money order or certified check.

RECORDING THE DEATH CERTIFICATE

In Arizona, the Department of Health Services issues the death certificate. The Department does not publish the death certificate so it is not part of the public record. If the decedent owned real property in Arizona, then it is important to record the decedent's death certificate in each county in which the decedent owned property.

If the deed to real property is in the name of a husband and his wife with rights of survivorship, then once the death certificate is recorded any one who examines the county record will know that the surviving spouse now owns the property. If, however, the decedent owned the property in his name only, then some sort of probate procedure will be necessary so that a new deed can be recorded to establish the identity of the new owner of the property.

In Arizona, the County Recorder in the county where the property is located, will record a certified copy of the death certificate. Call the County Recorder and ask where to mail the death certificate and how much money you need to send for the recording fee. Enclose a self addressed stamped envelop for the County Recorder to return the recorded death certificate to you so that you will have a record of where the certificate was recorded. If you intend to sell the property in the near future, then read Page 89 for other documents you may want to record at this time.

If the decedent owned property in another state, then a death certificate should be recorded in the county where that property is located. In some states the Clerk of the Circuit Court or the County Registrar is in charge of recording deeds (and death certificates). You will need to call the county clerk for information about how to record the death certificate in that county.

About Probate

Once a person dies, all of the property he owns as of the date of his death is referred to as the **decedent's estate.** If the decedent owned property that was in his name only (not jointly or in trust for someone) then some sort of court procedure is necessary to determine who is entitled to possession of the property. The name of the court procedure is **probate.**

There are different ways to conduct a probate procedure depending on the value of the probate estate and whether the decedent owned real property at the time of his death. The method of conducting a probate procedure is call the **estate administration**. Chapter 6 explains how to determine whether a probate procedure is necessary and if so, then what kind of estate administration is necessary.

The root of the word probate is "to prove." It refers to the first job of the probate court, that is, to examine proof of whether the decedent left a valid Will or whether the decedent died **intestate** (without a Will). The second job of the probate court is to appoint someone to wrap up the affairs of the decedent — to pay any outstanding bills and then to distribute what property is left to the beneficiaries. In Arizona, the person appointed by the probate court to do this job is called the **Personal Representative**.

The Personal Representative's first order of business is to give notice of the death. That procedure is explained in the next chapter.

CHAPTER 2
GIVING NOTICE OF THE DEATH

Those closest to the decedent usually notify family members and close friends by telephone. The funeral director will arrange to publish an obituary in as many different newspapers as the family requests, but there is still the job of notifying the government and people who were doing business with the decedent. That task belongs to the person named as Personal Representative (or Executor) in the decedent's Will. If the decedent died without a Will then Arizona statute 14-2303 gives the spouse the right to be appointed as Personal Representative. If there is no spouse, or if the spouse is unable or unwilling to serve, then any one who has a right to inherit the decedent's property, can ask to be appointed by the Probate court to serve as Personal Representative.

If no probate procedure is necessary, the job of notifying people of the death and settling the decedent's affairs falls to his spouse; and in the absence of a spouse, to the decedent's next of kin. By *next of kin*, we mean those people who inherit the decedent's property according to the Arizona Law of Intestate Succession. That law is explained in Chapter 5: ARIZONA'S INTESTATE LAW.

The person who has the job of settling the decedent's estate should begin to give notice as soon as is practicable after the death. Two government agencies that need to be notified are the Social Security Administration and the IRS. This chapter gives their telephone number as well as those of all the other agencies that need to be notified.

NOTIFYING SOCIAL SECURITY

Many Funeral Directors will, as part of their service package, notify the Social Security Administration of the death. You may wish to check to see that this has been done. You can do so by calling **1-800-772-1213**. You will need to give the Social Security Administration the full legal name of the decedent as well as his social security number and date of birth.

| *Special Situation* | FOR DECEDENT RECEIVING SOCIAL SECURITY CHECKS |

If the decedent was receiving checks from Social Security, then you need to determine whether his last check needs to be returned to the Social Security Administration.

Each Social Security check is a payment for the prior month, provided that person lives for the entire prior month. If someone dies on the last day of the month, then you should not cash the check for that month. For example, if someone dies on July 31st, then you need to return the check that the agency mails out in August. If however, the decedent died on August 1st then the check sent in August need not be returned because that check is payment for the month of July.

If the Social Security check is electronically deposited into a bank account then notify the bank that the account holder died and notify the Social Security Administration as well. If the check needs to be returned, then the Social Security Administration will withdraw it electronically from the bank account. You will need to keep the account open until the funds are withdrawn.

When Someone Dies In Arizona

 **SPOUSE**

SPOUSE AND CHILD'S SOCIAL SECURITY BENEFITS

If the decedent had sufficient work credits, the Social Security Administration will give the decedent's widow(er) or if unmarried, then the decedent's minor children, a one-time death benefit in the amount of $255.

SURVIVORS BENEFITS:

The spouse (or ex-spouse) of the decedent may be eligible for Survivors Benefits. Benefits vary depending on the amount of work credits earned by the decedent; whether the decedent had minor or disabled children; the spouse's age; how long they were married; etc.

The minor child of the decedent may be eligible for dependent child's benefits regardless of whether the decedent father ever married the child's mother. Paternity can be established by any one of several methods including the father acknowledging his child in writing or verbally to members of his family.

SOCIAL SECURITY BENEFITS

A spouse or ex-spouse can collect social security benefits based on the decedent's work record. This value may be greater than the spouse now receives. It is important to make an appointment with your local Social Security office and determine whether you as the spouse (or ex-spouse), or parent of the decedent's minor child, are eligible for Social Security or Survivor benefits. The SOCIAL SECURITY ADMINISTRATION has a web site from which you can down load publications that explain social security and survivor benefits.

    SOCIAL SECURITY WEB SITE
http://www.ssa.gov

> *Special Situation* DECEDENT WITH GOVERNMENT PENSION

If the decedent received a government pension then any check received after the date of death needs to be returned to the U.S. Treasury. If the check is direct deposited to a bank account, then call the financial institution and ask them to return the check. If the check is sent by mail then you need to return it to:

Director, Regional Finance Center
U. S. Treasury Department
P.O. Box 7367
Chicago, IL 60680

Include a letter explaining the reason for the return of the check and stating the decedent's date of death.

$$$ APPLY FOR BENEFITS $$$

Even though you notify the government of the death, they will not automatically give you benefits to which you may be entitled. You need to apply for those benefits by notifying the Office of Personnel Management ("OPM") of the death and requesting that they send you an application for survivor benefits. You can call them at 1-888-767-6738 or you can write to: THE OFFICE OF PERSONNEL MANAGEMENT SERVICE
AND RECORDS CENTER
BOYERS, PA 16017

OPM WEB SITE
You can get assistance via E-mail at
retire@opm.gov

You will find brochures and information about Survivor's Benefits at http://www.opm.gov

In most cases, pension and annuity checks are payment for the prior month. If the decedent received his pension or annuity check before his death, then no monies need be returned. Pension checks and/or annuity checks received after the date of death may need to be returned to the company. You need to notify the company of the death to determine the status of the last check sent to the decedent.

Before notifying the company, locate the policy or pension statement that is the basis of the income. That document should tell whether there is a beneficiary of the pension or annuity funds now that the pensioner or annuitant is dead. If you cannot locate the document, use the return address on the check envelope and ask the company to send you a copy of the plan. Also request that they forward to you any claim form that may be required in order for the survivor or beneficiary to receive benefits under that pension plan or policy.

If the pension/annuity check is direct deposited to the decedent's account, then ask the bank to assist you in locating the company and notifying the company of the death.

Special Situation	DECEDENT WITH AN INDIVIDUAL RETIREMENT ACCOUNT ("IRA") or a QUALIFIED RETIREMENT PLAN ("QRP")

Anyone who is a beneficiary of an IRA or QRP needs to keep in mind that, for some plans, no income taxes have been paid on monies placed in an IRA or QRP account. In such accounts, once monies are withdrawn, significant taxes may be due. You need to learn what options are available to you as a beneficiary of the plan and the tax consequences of each option. You will need to ask an accountant how much will be due in taxes for each option. Once you know all the facts, you will be able to make the best choice for your circumstance.

SPOUSE

If the spouse is the beneficiary of the decedent's IRA account, then there are special options available. The spouse has the right to withdraw the money from the account or roll it over into the spouse's own retirement account. There is a new type of IRA account available, called the ROTH IRA. Monies placed into the account have no tax break going in, but can be removed without paying any tax in the future. The spouse still needs to understand the tax consequence of choosing any given option. It is important to consult with an accountant to determine the best way to go.

If the decedent had a QRP, the plan may permit the spouse to roll the balance of the account into a new IRA. The spouse needs to contact the decedent's employer for an explanation of the plan and all the options that are available at this time, and of course, the spouse needs to consult with an accountant before choosing any option.

NOTIFYING IRS

THE FINAL INCOME TAX RETURN

The Personal Representative, or next of kin, needs to file the decedent's final state and federal income tax returns. This can be done as part of the income tax return for the year of his death. If you have a joint bank account with the decedent, do not close that account until you determine whether the decedent is entitled to an income tax refund. See Chapter 6 for an explanation of how to obtain a refund from the IRS and from the state.

THE GOOD NEWS

Monies inherited from the decedent are not counted as income to you, so you do not pay federal income tax on those monies. If the monies you inherit later earn interest or income for you, then of course you will report that income as you do any other type of income.

Real and personal property inherited by a beneficiary is inherited at a "stepped up" basis. This means that if the decedent purchased some item that is now worth more than when he purchased it, then the beneficiary inherits the property at its fair market value as of the decedent's date of death. For example, suppose the decedent bought stock for $20,000 and it is now worth $50,000, then the beneficiary inherits the stock at the $50,000 value If the beneficiary sells the stock for $50,000, he pays no tax. If the beneficiary holds onto the stock and later sells it for $60,000, the beneficiary will pay federal capital gains tax only on the $10,000 increase in value since the decedent's death.

WHEN TO EVALUATE THE PROPERTY

The IRS gives you a choice of taking the value of the decedent's property as of his date of death or 6 months later. For example, suppose you inherit stock certificates worth $50,000 and you decide to hold onto them. If they increase in value so that 6 months later they are worth $60,000, you can (by filing the proper IRS tax return) elect to take the six-month value in place of the date-of-death value. If you sell the stock at that time then you will not pay capital gains on the stock.

CAUTION If you hold onto the stock there is a risk that it will decrease in value during that six month period. If the stock goes down to $40,000, and you then sell, your only consolation will be that you can evaluate the stock as of the date of death and reflect the loss on your income tax statement.

Also, you need to consider the cost of employing an accountant to file the necessary forms for the 6-month election. If you hold onto the stock and the increase in value is only a few thousand dollars, it may not pay to take the election. The cost in time and expense to make the election may be more than the tax payment itself.

 SPOUSE

SPOUSE'S HOMESTEAD TAX BENEFITS

If the decedent's spouse owns an Arizona residence then the spouse may be eligible for a widow(er)'s tax exemption. Arizona statute 42-11111 gives a tax exemption for widows, widowers and disabled persons. There are residency requirements as well as income and value of the property requirements (assessed value of the property cannot exceed $10,000). You will need to contact the county assessor's office and request information about eligibility for the exemption. Application must be made between the first Monday in January and March 1st, else you lose the exemption for that year (AZ 42-11153). You can find the telephone number for the county assessor's office by looking under the county of the decedent's residence.

CAPITAL GAINS EXCLUSION

In the tough "ole days" the IRS used to allow a once-in-a-lifetime, over age 55, up to $125,000 capital gains tax exclusion on the sale of the homestead. If a married couple sold their home and took the exclusion it was "used up" and no longer available to the other partner. In these, the good times, the IRS allows you to sell your homestead and up to $500,000 of the home-sale profit is tax free (IRC Section 121 B 3). There is no limit on the number of times you can use the exemption, provided you live in the homestead at least 2 years prior to the sale.

If the decedent and his spouse used their "once in a lifetime" homestead tax exemption, with this new law, the surviving spouse can sell the homestead and once again take advantage of a tax break.

An *estate tax* is a tax imposed by the federal and state government for the transfer of property at death. The *taxable estate* of the decedent is the total value of all of his property, as of his date of death. This includes real property (homestead, vacant lots, etc.) and personal property (cars, life insurance policies, business interests, securities, IRA accounts, etc.). It includes property held in the decedent's name alone, as well as property that he held jointly or in trust for another.

The Federal government gives each person an Estate and Gift Tax Unified Credit. The state of Arizona allows the same estate tax credit. The credit applies to the decedent's taxable estate as well as gifts given during his lifetime that exceed $10,000/per person in any given year. The Unified Credit amount is scheduled to increase each year until the year 2006:

YEAR	TAXABLE ESTATE
2000 — 2001	$675,000
2002 — 2003	$700,000
2004	$850,000
2005	$950,000
2006	$1,000,000

No Arizona Estate tax return or Federal Estate tax return need be filed unless the decedent's taxable estate and lifetime gifts exceed the scheduled amount as of his date of death. If it does, then you need to employ an accountant to prepare an Estate tax return (IRS form 706) and Arizona Estate tax return form 76.

DECEDENT WITH A TRUST

If the decedent was the Grantor or Settlor of a trust, then the trust probably directs the Successor Trustee to do certain things upon the decedent's death. The trust document may instruct the Successor Trustee to make certain gifts when the Grantor or Settlor dies or the trust document may direct the Successor Trustee to hold money in trust for a beneficiary of the trust.

 IF YOU ARE
SUCCESSOR TRUSTEE

If you are the Successor Trustee then in addition to following the terms of the trust, you are required to obey all of the laws of the state of Arizona relating to the administration of a trust. For example, Arizona statute 14-7303(1) requires that within 30 days, you give written notice of your acceptance of the trust, to the beneficiaries of the trust who are entitled to the income from the trust. You should consult with an attorney experienced in Estate Planning to explain how to properly administer the trust and to ensure that you do so without any liability to yourself.

IF YOU ARE A BENEFICIARY

If you are a beneficiary of the trust, then you need to obtain a copy of the trust and see how the trust is to be administered now that the Grantor or Settlor is deceased. Arizona statute 14-7303 (2) requires that the Successor Trustee give a copy of the trust, and information about the trust assets, to a beneficiary, if he /she requests it. Most trust documents are written in "legalese," so you may want to employ your own attorney to review the trust, and explain what rights you have under that trust.

NOTIFYING THE BUSINESS COMMUNITY

People and companies who were doing business with the decedent need to be notified of his death. This includes utility companies, credit card companies, banks, brokerage firms and any company that insured the decedent.

If you hold a credit card jointly with the decedent, then it is important to waste no time in closing that account and opening another in your name only. Consider the case of Barbara and John. They never married but they did live together for several years before he died from AIDS. John came from a well to do family so he had enough money to support himself and Barbara during his illness. John put Barbara on all of his credit card accounts so that she could purchase things when he became too ill to go shopping with her. After the funeral, Barbara had a gathering of John's friends and family at their apartment. Barbara was so preoccupied with her loss that she never noticed that John's credit cards were missing.

Barbara did not know who ran up the bills on John's credit cards during the month following his death. It was obvious that John's signature had been forged — but who forged it? One credit card company suspected that it might have been Barbara herself. Because the cards were held jointly, Barbara became liable to either pay the debts or prove that she did not make the purchases. She was able to clear her credit record but it took several months and she had to employ an attorney to do so.

NOTIFY INSURANCE COMPANIES

Examine the decedent's financial records to determine the name and telephone number of all of the companies that insured the decedent or his property. This includes real property insurance, motor vehicle insurance, health insurance and life insurance.

MOTOR VEHICLE INSURANCE

If the decedent owned any type of motor vehicle (car, truck, boat, airplane) locate the insurance policy on that vehicle and notify the insurance company of the death. Determine how long insurance coverage continues after the death. Ask the insurance agent to explain what things are covered under the policy. Is the motor vehicle covered for all types of casualty (theft, accident, vandalism, etc.) or is coverage limited in some way? If you can continue coverage then determine when the next insurance payment is due. Hopefully, the car will be sold or transferred to a beneficiary before that date, but if not, then you need to arrange to continue with insurance coverage.

 **ACCIDENT INSURANCE**

If the decedent died as a result of an accident, then check for all possible sources of accident insurance coverage including his homeowner's policy. Some credit card companies provide free accident insurance as part of their contract with their card holders. If the decedent died in a car accident, then check to see whether he was covered by any type of travel insurance, such as rental car insurance. If he belonged to an automobile club, such as AAA, then check whether he had accident insurance as part of his club membership.

LIFE INSURANCE

If the decedent had life insurance, then you need to locate the policy and notify the company of his death. Call each life insurance company and ask what they require in order to forward the insurance proceeds to the beneficiary. Most companies will ask you to send them the original policy and a certified copy of the death certificate.

Send the original policy by certified mail or any of the overnight services that require a signed receipt for the package. Make a copy of the original policy for your records before mailing the original policy to the company.

IF YOU CANNOT LOCATE THE POLICY

If you know that the decedent was insured but you cannot locate the insurance policy, the AMERICAN COUNCIL OF LIFE INSURANCE ("ACLI") may be able to help you. Write to the ACLI giving them the name, address, date of birth, and social security number of the decedent. Their address is:

POLICY SEARCH ACLI
1000 Pennsylvania Avenue, NW
Washington, DC 20004

The ACLI will assist you by asking the 100 largest insurance companies in the nation to search their records for the missing policy. If it is found, you will receive a copy of the policy free of charge.

IF YOU CANNOT LOCATE THE COMPANY

If you cannot locate the insurance company it may be doing business under another name or it may no longer be doing business in the state of Arizona. Insurance companies are highly regulated. Each state has a branch of government that regulates insurance companies. If you are having difficulty locating the insurance company call the Department of Insurance in the state where the policy was purchased and ask for assistance in locating the company. The number for **THE ARIZONA DEPARTMENT OF INSURANCE** is 800-325-2548.

 EAGLE PUBLISHING COMPANY OF BOCA's web site gives the telephone number of the Department of Insurance for each state: http://www.eaglepublishing.com

COMPANY INSURANCE

If the decedent was employed then his employer may provide survivor benefits from a company or group life insurance plan and/or a retirement plan. If the decedent belonged to a union, then check with the union to determine whether members of the union receive any death benefits.

The decedent may have belonged to a professional, fraternal or social organization such as the local Chamber of Commerce, a Veteran's organization, the Kiwanis, AARP, the Rotary Club, etc. If he belonged to such an organization check to see whether the organization provided any type of insurance coverage.

If the decedent owned his own company he may have purchased "key man" insurance. Key man insurance is designed to protect the company against the loss of a valuable employee. Benefits are paid to the company to compensate the company for the loss of someone who is essential to the continuation of the business. Ultimately the policy benefits those who inherit the business.

If the decedent owned shares in the company or was a partner in the company, there may be a shareholder's agreement or partnership agreement that requires the company to use the key man insurance proceeds to purchase the shares or buy out the partnership interest owned by the decedent. If there is a probate procedure, then the Personal Representative's attorney will review the agreement. If the decedent died without a Will, then the next of kin needs to investigate the matter to determine what rights (if any) the family has to the proceeds of the key man insurance policy.

DECEDENT OWNER OR STATUTORY AGENT OF A CORPORATION

If the decedent was the sole owner and officer of a corporation then the Arizona Corporation Commission needs to be notified of the change. There may need to be a probate procedure to determine the new owner of the company so it may take some period of time before new officers and directors are identified.

If the decedent was the statutory agent of a corporation, then a new agent needs to be appointed and the Commission advised of the change. Forms to change officers and statutory agents can be obtained by calling the Arizona Corporation Commission at (602) 542-3026.

Arizona statute 10-502 allows the change to be made as part of the next annual report so if the change is not made sooner, it can be done at the same time the annual report is filed.

STATUS REPORT

If you were not actively involved in running the business, then you might request a status report of the company. The report will show whether filing fees are current and will identify the officers and directors of the company.

```
┌─────────────────────────────────────────┐
│        NOTIFY THE CONDOMINIUM             │
│     OR HOMEOWNERS  ASSOCIATION            │
└─────────────────────────────────────────┘
```

If the decedent owned a condominium or a residence regulated by a homeowner's association, then the association needs to be notified of the death. Once the property is transfered to the proper beneficary, he/she will need to contact the association and arrange to have notices of dues or assessments forwarded to the new owner.

HOMEOWNER'S INSURANCE
If the decedent owned his own home, then check whether there is sufficient insurance coverage on the property. The decedent may have neglected to increase his insurance as the property appreciated in value.   If you think the property may be vacant for some period of time, then consider having vandalism coverage included in the policy. Once the property is sold, or transferred to the proper beneficiary, you can have the policy discontinued or transferred to the new owner. The decedent's estate should receive a rebate for the unused portion of the premium.

MORTGAGE INSURANCE
If the decedent had a mortgage on any parcel of real estate that he owned, he might have arranged with his lender for an insurance policy that pays off the mortgage balance in the event of his death.   Look at the closing statement to see if there was a charge for mortgage insurance.   Also, check with the lender to determine if such a policy was purchased.

If the decedent was the sole owner of the property, then the Personal Representative (or beneficiary) of that property needs to make arrangements to continue payment of the mortgage until title to the property is transferred to that beneficiary.

HEALTH INSURANCE

The Health Insurance carrier probably knows of the death, but it is a good idea to contact them to determine what coverage the decedent had under that insurance plan. If you cannot find the original policy, have the insurance company send you a copy of the policy so that you can determine whether medical treatment rendered to the decedent before his death was covered by that policy.

 *Special Situation* → **DECEDENT ON MEDICARE**

If the decedent was insured under Medicare, you can determine what services are covered by that plan by writing to: U.S. GOVERNMENT PRINTING OFFICE
U.S. Dept. of Health and Human Services
Health Care Financing Administration
7500 Security Boulevard
Baltimore, MD 21244-1850
and asking for the U. S Printing Office Publication Number HCFA 10050: YOUR MEDICARE HANDBOOK. You can find YOUR MEDICARE HANDBOOK and other information about other Health Care Financing Administration publications at the HCFA Web site:

 HCFA WEB SITE
http://www.hcfa.gov

There is a toll-free Medicare Hotline 1-800-633-4227. English and Spanish speaking operators are available Monday through Friday from 8 a.m. to 4:30 p.m TTY/TDD service for the hearing impaired is available toll free at 1-877-486-2048.

 SPOUSE

THE SPOUSE'S HEALTH INSURANCE

If the spouse of the decedent is insured under Medicare, then the death does not affect the surviving spouse's coverage. If the spouse was not covered by Medicare but had his/her own policy that also insured the decedent, the spouse needs to notify the employer of the death because this may affect the cost of the plan to the employer and/or the spouse.

If the spouse was covered under the decedent's policy then he/she needs to arrange for new coverage. If the decedent was employed by a federally regulated company (usually a company with at least twenty employees) then under the Consolidated Omnibus Budget Reconciliation Act ("COBRA") the employer must make the company health plan available to the surviving spouse and any dependent child of the decedent for at least 36 months. The employer is required to give notice to the surviving spouse and/or dependent child of their right to continue coverage under the decedent's health plan.

SPOUSE'S HEALTH INSURANCE
(continued)

The spouse or dependent child has 60 days from the date of death or 60 days after notice is sent by the employer (whichever is later) to notify the employer whether they wish to continue under the plan. The only problem with continued coverage may be the cost. Before the death, the employer may have been paying some percentage of the premium. The employer has no such duty after the death unless there was some employment agreement stating otherwise. Under COBRA, the employer may charge the spouse for the full cost of the plan plus a 2% administrative fee.

You can find additional information about COBRA in the publication PENSION AND HEALTH CARE COVERAGE. This and other publications from the U.S. Department of Labor can be found at their web site:

 Department of Labor Web Site
http://www.dol.gov/dol/pwba

✍ CHANGE BENEFICIARY ✍

If the decedent was someone that you named as your beneficiary in an insurance policy, security, Will or pension plan, then you may need to name another beneficiary in his place:

INSURANCE POLICY ✍

If you named the decedent as the primary beneficiary of your life insurance policy, then check to see whether you named an alternate beneficiary in the event that the decedent did not survive you. If not, then you need to contact the insurance company to name a new beneficiary at this time.

WILL OR TRUST ✍

Most Wills provide for an alternate beneficiary in the event that the person named as beneficiary dies first. If you named the decedent as your beneficiary, then check to see whether you named an alternate beneficiary. If not, you will need to have your attorney prepare a codicil (addendum) to your Will.

Similarly, if you are the Grantor or Settlor of a trust and the decedent was one of the beneficiaries of your trust, then check the trust document to see if you named an alternate beneficiary. If not, contact your attorney to prepare an amendment to the trust, naming a new beneficiary.

BANK/SECURITIES ACCOUNT ✍

If the decedent was a beneficiary of your bank or securities account, or if the decedent was a joint owner of your bank account or securities account, then it is important to contact the financial institution and inform them of the death. You may wish to arrange for a new beneficiary or joint owner at this time.

PENSION PLANS ✍

If the decedent was a beneficiary under your pension plan, then you need to notify them of his death and name a new beneficiary. Many pension plans require that you notify them within a set period of time (usually 30 days) so it is important to notify them as soon as you are able.

If the decedent was a beneficiary of your Individual Retirement Account ("IRA") or of your Qualified Retirement Plan ("QRP") and you did not provide for an alternate beneficiary, then you need to name someone at this time.

There are many government regulations relating to IRA and QRP accounts. For example, you must begin to withdraw money from the account once you reach the age of 70 1/2. How much you must withdraw depends on whether you choose to base the amount withdrawn on your own life expectancy or on the joint life expectancy of you and your oldest beneficiary.

If you have not reached the age of 70 1/2, then before naming a new beneficiary, you may wish to consult with your accountant to decide what is the best option for you.

NOTIFYING CREDITORS

If the decedent owed money, and a probate procedure is necessary, then it will be the job of the person who is appointed as Personal Representative to give written notice of the death to all of the decedent's creditors. The attorney who handles the probate will explain to the Personal Representative how notice is to be given.

If no probate procedure is necessary, then the next of kin can notify the creditors of the death, but before doing so, first read Chapter 4: WHAT BILLS NEED TO BE PAID?

LOCATING THE DECEDENT'S ASSETS

Chapter 4 of this book explains what bills need to be paid and who is responsible to pay them, but before any bill can be paid, you need to know what the decedent owned as of his date of death. The next chapter explains how to identify, and then locate all of the property owned by the decedent.

It is important to locate the financial records of the decedent and then carefully examine those records. Even the partner of a long-term marriage should conduct a thorough search because the surviving spouse may be unaware of all that was owned (or owed) by the decedent.

It is not unusual for a surviving spouse to be surprised when learning of the decedent's business transactions — especially in those cases where the decedent had control of family finances. One such example is that of Sam and Henrietta. They married just as soon as Sam was discharged from the army after World War II. During their marriage, Sam handled all of the finances, giving Henrietta just enough money to run the household.

Every now and again Henrietta would think of getting a job. She longed to have her own source of income and some economic independence. Each time she brought up the subject Sam would loudly object. He had no patience for this new "woman's lib" thing. Sam said he got married to have a real wife — one who would cook his meals and keep house for him.

Henrietta was not the arguing type. She rationalized, saying that Sam had a delicate stomach and dust allergies. He needed her to prepare his special meals and keep an immaculate house for him. Besides, Sam had a good job with a major cruise line and he needed her to accompany him on his frequent business trips.

Once Sam retired, he was even more cautious in his spending habits. Henrietta seldom complained. She assumed the reason for his "thrift" was that they had little money and had to live on his pension. They were married for 52 years when Sam died at the age of 83. Henrietta was 81 at the time of his death. She was one very happy, very angry and very aged widow when she discovered that Sam left her with assets worth well over a million dollars!

LOCATING FINANCIAL RECORDS

To locate the decedent's assets you need to find evidence of what he owned and where those assets are located. His financial records should lead you to the location of all of his assets so your first job is to locate those records. The best place to start the search is in the decedent's home. Many people keep their financial records in a single place but it is important to check the entire house to be sure you did not miss something.

CHECK THE COMPUTER
Don't overlook that computer sitting silently in the corner. It may hold the decedent's check register and all of the decedent's financial records. The computer may be programmed to protect information. If you cannot access the decedent's records, you may need to employ a computer technician or computer consultant who will be able to print out all of the information on the hard drive of the computer. You can find such a technician or consultant by looking in the telephone book under
COMPUTER SUPPORT SERVICES or
COMPUTER SYSTEM DESIGNS & CONSULTANTS.

COLLECT AND IDENTIFY KEYS

The decedent may have kept his records in a safe deposit box, so you may find that your first job is to locate the keys to the box. As you go through the personal effects of the decedent, collect and identify all the keys that you find. If you come across an unidentified key, it could be a key to a post office box (private or federal) or a safe deposit box located in a bank or in a private vault company. You will need to determine whether that key opens a box that contains property belonging to the decedent or whether the key is to a box no longer in use. Some ways to investigate are as follows:

☑ CHECK BUSINESS RECORDS

If the decedent kept receipts, look through those items to see if he paid for the rental of a post office or safe deposit box. Also, check his check register to see if he wrote out a check to the Postmaster or to any safe deposit or vault company. Look at his bank statements to see if there is any bank charge for a safe deposit box. Some banks bill separately for safe deposit boxes so check with all of the banks in which the decedent had an account to determine if he had a box with that bank.

☑ CHECK THE KEY TYPE

If you cannot identify a safe deposit box key that you found, take it a local locksmith and ask whether they can identify the type of facility that uses such keys. If that doesn't work then go to each bank, post office and private safe deposit boxes located in places where the decedent shopped, worked or frequented and ask whether they use that type of key.

☑ CHECK THE MAIL

Check the mail over the next several months to see if the decedent receives a statement requesting payment for the next year's rental of a post office or safe deposit box.

FORWARD THE DECEDENT'S MAIL

You may find evidence of a brokerage account, bank account, or safe deposit box by examining correspondence addressed to the decedent. If the decedent was living alone, then have the mail forwarded to the person he named as Personal Representative or executor of his Will. If the decedent did not leave a Will then the mail should be forwarded to his next of kin. Call the Postmaster and ask him/her to send you the necessary forms to make the change. Request that the mail be forwarded for the longest period allowed by law (currently one year).

The decedent may have been renting a post office box at his local post office branch or perhaps at the branch closest to where he did his banking. Ask the Postmaster to help you determine whether the decedent was renting a post office box. If so, then you need to locate the key to the box so that you can collect the decedent's mail.

Special Situation ▷ LOST POST OFFICE BOX KEY

If the decedent had a post office box and you cannot locate the key, then contact the local postmaster and ask him/her what documentation is needed for you to gain possession of the mail in that box. As before, you will ask the Postmaster to have all future mail addressed to that box, forwarded to the Personal Representative, or if there is no Will, then to the decedent's next of kin.

When Someone Dies In Arizona

WHAT TO DO WITH CHECKS

You may receive checks in the mail made out to the decedent. Social security checks, pension checks and annuity checks issued after the date of death need to be returned to the sender (see pages 26 and 28 of this book). Other checks need to be deposited to the decedent's bank account. The decedent is not here to endorse the check, but you can deposit to his account by writing his bank account number on the back of the check and printing beneath it "**FOR DEPOSIT ONLY.**" The bank will accept such an endorsement and deposit the check into the decedent's account. If the check is significant in value and/or the decedent had different accounts that are accessible to different people, then there needs to be cooperation and a sense of fair play. If not, the dollar gain may not nearly offset the emotional turmoil. Such was the case with Gail.

Gail's father made her a joint owner of his checking account to assist in paying his bills. He had macular degeneration and it was increasingly difficult for him to see. The father also had a savings account that was in his name only.

Gail's brother, Richard, had a good paying job in Canada. Even though he lived at a distance, Richard, his wife and two children always spent the holidays with his father. Gail's good cooking added to the festivities. Summers were still another time for a visit with Richard and his family. Their father enjoyed leaving the heat of Arizona to spend a few weeks with Richard in the cool Canadian climate.

One July, the father purchased a round trip ticket to Canada. It cost several hundred dollars. Just before the departure date, the father had a heart attack and died.

Gail called the airline to cancel the ticket. They refunded the money in a check made out to her father. She deposited the check into the joint account.

As part of the probate procedure, the money in the father's savings account was divided equally between Richard and his sister. Richard wondered what happened to the money from the airline tickets. Gail explained "He paid for the tickets from the joint account, so I deposited the money back to the joint account. "

"Well aren't you going to give me half?"

"Dad meant for me to have whatever was in that joint account. If he wanted you to have half of the money, he would have made you joint owner as well."

Richard didn't see it that way:
"That refund was part of Dad's probate estate. It should have been deposited to his savings account to be divided equally between us. Are you going to force me to argue this in court?"

Gail finally agreed to split the money with Richard, but the damage was done.

Gail complains that holidays are lonely since her father died.

LOCATE OUT OF STATE ACCOUNTS

If the decedent had out of state bank or brokerage accounts, then you might be able to locate them if they mail the decedent monthly or quarterly statements. Not all institutions do so, but all institutions are required to send out an IRS tax form 1099 each year giving the amount of interest earned on that account. Once those forms come in, you will learn the location of all of the decedent's active accounts.

COLLECT LEGAL DOCUMENTS

As you go through the papers of the decedent you may come across documents that indicate property ownership, such as bank registers, title to motor vehicles, stock or bond certificates, insurance policies, brokerage account statements, etc. Place all evidence of ownership in a single place. You will need to contact different institutions to transfer title to the proper beneficiary. Chapter 5 explains how to identify the proper beneficiary. Chapter 6 explains how to transfer the property to that beneficiary.

COLLECT DEEDS

Collect the deeds to all property owned by the decedent. Many people keep deeds in a safe deposit box. If you cannot find the deed in the decedent's home, then you need to determine whether he had a safe deposit box. If you know that the decedent owned real property (lot, residence, condominium, cooperative, time share, etc.) but you cannot locate the deed, then contact the County Recorder, in the county in which the property is located, and ask for a copy of the deed.

You will need to identify the parcel of land by giving the legal description of the land or its parcel identification number. You can find this information on the last tax bill sent to the decedent. If you cannot find the last tax bill, then call the County Assessor's office and they will give you the information.

You can use the same procedure if you cannot locate the deed to property owned by the decedent in another state, namely, check with the recording department in the county where the property is located. Some states keep their land records in the court house. If such is the case, then check with the Clerk of the County Court or the Clerk of the Circuit Court.

LOCATE CONTRACTS

If the decedent belonged to a health club or gym, he may have prepaid for the year. Look for the club contract. It will give the terms of the agreement. If you cannot locate the contract then contact the company for a copy of the agreement. If the contract was prepaid, then determine whether the agreement provides for a refund for the unused portion.

 **RESIDENTIAL LEASE**

If the decedent was renting his residence, then he may have a lease agreement. It is important to locate the lease because the decedent's estate may be responsible for payments under the lease. If you cannot find a lease, then ask the landlord for a copy. If the landlord reports that there was no lease, then verify with the landlord that the decedent was on a month to month basis. You will need to work out a schedule to vacate the premises.

If a written lease is in effect, then determine the end of the lease period. If that date is more than a couple of months away, then ask the landlord whether he will agree to cancel the lease on the condition that the property is vacated in good condition. If the landlord wants to hold the estate liable for the balance of the lease, then it is prudent to have an attorney review the lease to determine what rights and responsibilities remain now that the tenant is deceased.

☎ LAWYER | ONGOING BUSINESS

If the decedent had his own business or was a partner or shareholder of a small company, then the Personal Representative (or next of kin, if he died intestate) needs to contact the company accountant to obtain the company's business records. If there is a company attorney, then contact the attorney for assistance in continuing to operate the business or terminating it. If you are a beneficiary of the estate, consider consulting with your own attorney to determine your rights and responsibilities in the business.

COLLECT TAX RECORDS

You will need to file the decedent's final state and federal income tax return so you need to collect all of his tax records that he filed for the past 3 years. If you cannot locate his prior tax records, then check his personal telephone book and/or his personal bank register to see if he employed an accountant. If you can locate his accountant, then contact the accountant to see if he/she has a copy of those records.

If you are unable to locate the decedent's federal tax records then they can be obtained from the IRS. The IRS will send copies of the decedent's tax filings to anyone who has a *fiduciary relationship* with the decedent. The IRS considers the following people to be fiduciaries:

➤ the person named as personal representative (or executor) of the decedent's Will

➤ the successor trustee of the decedent's trust

➤ if the person died intestate, then whoever is legally entitled to possession of the decedent's property (See Chapter 5 to learn who are the beneficiaries.)

To notify the IRS of the fiduciary capacity, you need to file Form 56: NOTICE CONCERNING FIDUCIARY RELATIONSHIP
To request the copies, file IRS Form 4506:
    REQUEST FOR COPY OR TRANSCRIPT OF TAX FORM
Your accountant can file these forms for you or you can obtain the forms from the IRS by calling **1-800-829-3676**.

STATE INCOME TAX RETURN

If you cannot locate the decedent's state income tax return you can obtain copies from the Arizona Department of Revenue. There is a nominal charge of $1.00 for the first page and $0.10 for each additional page. It usually takes the department a month to process your request. To obtain the copies of the decedent's state income tax return, you will need to fill out a form entitled:
    Notice Of Assumption of Fiduciary Duties
and Arizona Form 450:
    Request for Certified Copies of Document.

To obtain a copy of these forms, call the state form order department at (602) 542-4260
or fax your request to (602) 542-3756 or you can write to:
    Arizona Department of Revenue
    Forms Order Department
    1600 W. Monroe
    Phoenix, AZ   85007-2650

ARIZONA DEPARTMENT OF REVENUE
WEB SITE
www.revenue.state.az.us

You can obtain information about Arizona's taxes from the Arizona Department of Revenue's Web Site. The web site does not contain tax forms that you can download at this time, but they might be available via the internet in the future.

FINDING LOST/ ABANDONED PROPERTY

If the decedent was aged and forgetful, he might have lost or abandoned property, such as a bank account, contents of a safe deposit box, a stock or brokerage account, travelers checks, pay checks, money orders, annuities, or insurance funds, etc. If property located in Arizona is unclaimed for more than 5 years then it is presumed to be abandoned. Such property is required to be turned over to the state who will, within 3 years, sell it at auction. (AZ 44-322). Once the property is sold, anyone who makes a valid claim for the property will receive the net proceeds of the sale. (AZ 44-324(C)).

You can determine whether there is a record identifying the decedent as the owner of abandoned property by calling (602) 542-4643 or by writing to:

THE DEPARTMENT OF REVENUE
UNCLAIMED PROPERTY UNIT
P.O. Box 29026
Phoenix, AZ   85038-9026

Each state has an agency or department that is responsible for handling lost, abandoned or unclaimed property located within that state. If the decedent had residences in other states, then call the comptroller's department in each of those states and check their UNCLAIMED or ABANDONED PROPERTY department to see if the decedent has unclaimed property in that state.

 EAGLE PUBLISHING COMPANY OF BOCA
lists telephone numbers for the
unclaimed property division for
each state on their web site:
www.eaglepublishing.com

LOCATING THE WILL

Arizona statute 14-2516 requires that the person who has the decedent's original Will must, upon the request of any interested person, deposit it with the court or with someone who can have the Will probated, such as the attorney for the named Personal Representative.

If you have possession of the original Will, you can deposit it with the Registrar of the Probate section of the Superior Court in the county in which the decedent lived. There is only one original Will, so it is important to hand carry the original document to the Registrar. If you are unable to make the delivery in person, you can mail the Will to the Registrar, but send it by certified mail so that you will have proof of delivery. Make a copy of the Will for your own records before delivering it to the court.

You may wish to call the clerk for directions to the Probate section, and also to learn of the the best time to meet with the clerk to avoid a wait in line.

 **LAWYER**

DECEDENT WITH OUT OF STATE RESIDENCE

If the decedent had his principal residence in another state, then before you deposit the Will, consult with an attorney experienced in Probate matters to determine whether the Will needs to be probated in Arizona or in the state of his residence. If the Will is to be probated in another state, then it is best to contact an attorney in that state and arrange to have the Will deposited with the Probate court in the state of his residence.

THE MISSING WILL

It is estimated that 70% of the population do not have a Will, so if you cannot find a Will, chances are that the decedent did not have one. If you think that the decedent had a Will, but you cannot find it, then try to locate the decedent's check book for the past few years and see whether he paid any attorney fees. If you are able to locate the decedent's attorney, then call and inquire whether the attorney ever drafted a Will for the decedent, and if so, whether the attorney has the original Will in his possession.

If the attorney has the original Will, then ask the attorney to forward the Will to the probate court. Asking the attorney to forward the Will to the court does not obligate you to employ the attorney should you later find that a formal probate procedure is necessary.

If you believe that the decedent had a Will but you cannot find it, then check to see if the decedent had a safe deposit box. If he did, you will need to gain entry to that box to see whether the Will is in the box. See the next page for an explanation of how to gain entry to the safe deposit box.

 A COPY AND NO ORIGINAL

If you have a copy of the Will but cannot locate the original then Arizona statute 14-3415 (B) allows the estate of the decedent to be probated using the copy, provided you can prove that the document is a true copy of the decedent's valid,unrevoked Will. You will need to employ an attorney who is experienced in probate matters to present such proof to the court.

ACCESSING THE SAFE DEPOSIT BOX

If the decedent had a safe deposit box and he was the only person with access to the safe deposit box, then Arizona statute 6-1008 gives any interested party (spouse, family member, person named in the Will, etc.) the right to go to the bank and ask the bank (or safe deposit box lessor) to allow them to examine the contents of the box. The statute requires that at least two company employees be present when the safe deposit box is opened.

If the Will is found in the box, then the bank will deliver it to the Clerk of the Superior Court. If the person named as Executor or Personal Representative is present, then the statute allows the bank to give the Will to that person. Also, if there is a life insurance policy in the safe deposit box the bank is authorized to give the policy to the beneficiary named in the policy. Nothing else may be removed from the safe deposit box until someone provides proof to the bank that he/she is legally entitled to take possession of the remaining contents of the safe deposit box. See Chapter 6 for an explanation of what type of probate procedure is necessary in order to get possession of the remaining items in the safe deposit box.

Before going to the bank, call ahead of time and make an appointment to meet with an officer of the company. Most companies require that you bring a certified copy of the death certificate, so you may need to wait until you receive the death certificate to prove to the bank officials that the owner of the box is dead.

Before leaving the bank, ask an officer of the company to make an inventory of the contents of the decedent's safe deposit box using the company letterhead. You may need the inventory to present to the court should you need an order to get possession of the contents of the box.

CHAPTER 4
WHAT BILLS NEED TO BE PAID?

Arizona is a state that respects the rights of creditors. If the estate of the decedent has sufficient assets, then the Personal Representative of the decedent's estate has the duty to be sure that all of the decedent's valid bills are paid. If the decedent had many debts, there may not be sufficient funds to pay all of the bills. The only remaining question is whether anyone else is responsible to pay those bills. If the decedent was married, then the first person the debtor will look to, is the decedent's spouse.

Historically, a husband was legally held responsible for his wife's debts — especially if those debts were for her basic necessities. Under the old English common law, once a woman married, her legal identity merged with that of her husband. A married woman had no right to own property or to enter into a contract in her own name. Once married, a woman became totally dependent on her husband and he was legally responsible to provide her with basic necessities — food, clothing, shelter and medical services. If anyone provided these necessities to his wife, then, regardless of whether the husband agreed to be responsible for the debt, he became obliged to pay for them. This law was called the DOCTRINE OF NECESSARIES.

The United States inherited its legal system from England, but over the years each state developed its own set of laws relating to spousal responsibility. Some states decided to make the Doctrine of Necessaries part of their state law. Other states, such as New Jersey, decided to apply the Doctrine equally to both sexes, making the husband responsible to pay for his wife's necessaries and the wife responsible to pay for her husband's necessaries. Other states, such as Florida, abolished the law altogether. In these states neither spouse is liable for the debts of the other unless the spouse agrees to pay the debt.

Arizona is a Community Property state. Whether the spouse is liable to pay the decedent's debts depends on whether the property owned by the surviving spouse is separate property or community property. Arizona statute 25-211 defines *community property* as all property that is acquired by either husband or wife during the marriage, except for property that either party inherits during the marriage or is given as a gift. The spouses have equal control of their community property (AZ 25-214).

Separate property is defined as anything owned by a spouse prior to marriage and anything acquired by a spouse during the marriage as a gift or an inheritance. Any profit or increase in value of separate property is also separate property (AZ 25-213). For example, if a husband owned rental property prior to his marriage, then any money he receives as rental is separate property. If the property appreciates in value, then that increase in value is also separate property. Of course if the increase in value of separate property is due to the efforts of the spouse, then the spouse is entitled to half of that increase in value.

COMMUNITY PROPERTY LIABILITY

If the surviving spouse agreed to be jointly responsible for a debt, then the surviving spouse must pay the debt from whatever assets he/she has, regardless of whether that property is separate property or community property.

If the surviving spouse did not agree to pay the decedent's debt, then whether the creditor can collect depends on whether the decedent had any separate property. If the decedent did not own separate property, then the creditor will look to the decedent's share of the community property for payment.

If all the surviving spouse owns is separate property then Arizona statute 25-215 (A) states that the creditor cannot force the surviving spouse to use those assets to pay the debt. But if there is community property available, then the surviving spouse must make the decedent's share of the community property available to pay his debts.

The decedent's share of the community property must be used to pay his debts even if the debts were incurred before the marriage, and even if the debts were incurred outside the state of Arizona. There are two limitations:
- ▷ the debt must have been incurred after 9/1/73
- ▷ the amount available to the decedent's creditor is limited to the amount the decedent contributed to the community property.

 **SIGNIFICANT DEBT AND COMMUNITY PROPERTY ONLY**

If the decedent left a significant amount of debt and only community property, then it is important to consult with an attorney to determine how much of the community property must be used to pay the debt. Theoretically, if the decedent came into the marriage with nothing and contributed little, then there is little, if any, community property available to pay his debts. No doubt a creditor will not see things that way. Regardless of the amount of the decedent's contribution it is best to consult with a Probate attorney to determine how much of the community funds are at risk.

NO COMMUNITY LIABILITY FOR OUT OF STATE TAXES ON PENSION

If the decedent retired to Arizona and was receiving a pension check, or monies from a retirement plan from another state, then Arizona statute 33-1151 protects those pension funds from any income tax that the other state might levy against those funds. The other state can get a judgment for taxes owed in that state on pension funds received by the decedent while he was a resident of Arizona, but they will not be able to collect on it in the state of Arizona. This protection extends to the spouse and any dependent of the decedent. Specifically, if the spouse or someone who was dependent on the decedent, inherits all of the decedent's property, then the other state will not be able to collect their income tax from that inheritance. This protection does not extend to anyone else. If the decedent was single and without any dependent, his out of state taxes can be collected from his estate.

NO COMMUNITY LIABILITY FOR MEDICAID

Medicaid is a program that provides medical and long term nursing care for people with low income and limited resources. The program is funded jointly by the federal and state government. Federal law 42 U.S.C. 1396(p) requires the state to put into effect a plan to recover monies spent from the estate of a deceased Medicaid recipient. If the decedent received long term medical assistance after January 1, 1994 or after he became 55, whichever is later, then the state of Arizona will seek to recover monies spent on his behalf. As a matter of public policy, the state does not seek recovery if the decedent has a surviving spouse, or a child who is disabled, or a child who is under 21. But they will try to recover if he had assets and was single without dependents.

The state does not require that a person sell his home to become eligible for Medicaid, but once he dies the state can make a *claim* (demand for payment) against his estate. Whoever inherits the decedent's home will need to settle with the state of Arizona before taking title to the property. If the decedent owned his home with another person as *joint tenants with rights of survivorship*, then the state cannot put a claim against that property because once the decedent dies, the joint tenant owns the property.

The recovery program is administered by the ARIZONA HEALTH CARE COST CONTAINMENT SYSTEM ("AHCCCS"). If you have a question about Medicaid claims against the decedent's estate you can call them at (602) 417-4000 or visit their web site:

AHCCCS WEB SITE
www.ahcccs.state.az.us.

JOINT DEBTS

A *joint debt* is a debt that two or more people are responsible to pay. Usually the contract or promissory note reads that both parties agree to *joint and severable* liability, meaning they both agree to pay the debt and each of them, individually, agree to be pay the debt. A joint debt can also be in the form of monies owed by one person with payment guaranteed by another person. If the person who owes the money does not pay, then the *guarantor* is responsible to pay the debt.

Before paying a bill, determine whether it is the decedent's debt or a joint debt. Hospital bills, nursing home bills, funeral expenses, legal fees incurred because of the decedent's death are all debts of the decedent's estate. They are not joint debts unless someone guaranteed payment for the monies owed.

DEBTS THE SPOUSE MUST PAY
Regardless of whether the surviving spouse has separate property or community property, loans signed by the decedent and his spouse are joint debts, as are charges on credit cards that both were authorized to use. Property taxes are a joint debt if the decedent and the spouse both owned the property.

PAYING FOR THE JOINT DEBT
If another person is jointly responsible for monies owed by the decedent, then that bill should be paid from any joint account held with the decedent. If the joint debtor did not have a joint account with the decedent, then the joint debtor must pay the bill from his/her own funds.

JOINT ACCOUNTS BUT NO JOINT DEBT

Suppose all of the decedent's funds are held jointly with his spouse or a family member and the joint owner of the account did not agree to pay those debts? Can the creditor require that half of the joint funds be set aside to pay the debt?

In Arizona, the answer is "Yes." Arizona statute 14-6215 states that if there isn't enough money in the decedent's estate to pay all his creditors and/or the statutory allowances to the surviving spouse and children, then the beneficiary must give the money from the decedent's share of a joint account to the decedent's Personal Representative to the extent those monies are needed to pay such debts. Similarly, if the decedent had an account and he gave written instructions to the bank to pay the money to a beneficiary when he dies (a *"pay on death"* or an *"in trust for"* account) then those funds can also be used to pay the decedent's creditors.

If the joint owner or beneficiary of the account takes the money and it is needed to pay the decedent's debts, then as much as is necessary to pay the debt must be returned.

There is no obligation to turn over these funds unless a creditor writes to the Personal Representative demanding that the monies from the account be used to pay the debt. Once the Personal Representative receives the demand, then unless the beneficiary agrees to return the funds, the Personal Representative will start a court proceeding to recover the funds. There is a one-year Statute of Limitations so if there is no court proceeding within a year from the decedent's date of death, the beneficiaries are free to keep the money.

NO MONEY — NO PROPERTY

If the decedent owed money then the bill needs to be paid from assets owned by the decedent — which leads to the next question "Did the decedent have any money in his name when he died?"

If the decedent died without any money or property then there is no money to pay any creditor. The only question that remains is whether anyone else is liable to pay those bills. As discussed previously, if the decedent was married then the creditor can look to community property held by the surviving spouse for payment. If the decedent was single, or if there is no community property, then the creditor has no means of being paid, but that usually does not stop them from asking for payment from the family.

The issue of payment most often arises in relation to services provided by nursing homes. When a person enters a nursing home, he is usually too ill to speak for himself or even sign his name. In such cases, the nursing home administrator will ask the spouse or a family member to sign a battery of papers on behalf of the patient before allowing the patient to enter the facility. Buried in that battery of papers may be a statement that the family member agrees to be responsible for payment to the nursing home. If the family member refuses to guarantee payment and the patient's finances are limited, then the facility may refuse to admit the patient.

If a nursing home accepts Medicare or Medicaid payments, then under the Federal Nursing Home Reform Law, that nursing home is prohibited from requiring a family member to guarantee payment as a condition of allowing the patient to enter that facility. USC Title 42 §1395I-3(c)(5)(A)(ii). Nonetheless, it is common practice for a nursing home, in effect, to say "Either someone agrees to pay for the patient's bill or you need to find a different facility."

Their position is understandable. Most nursing homes are business establishments and not charitable organizations. The nursing home must be paid for the services they provide or they soon will be out of business. For an insolvent patient, the solution to the problem is to have the patient admitted to a facility as a Medicaid patient.

But what if decedent had some money when he entered the nursing home and you agreed to guarantee payment to the nursing home?

What if you feel that you were coerced into signing as a guarantor?

Are you now liable to pay the decedent's final nursing home bill if your family member died without funds?

An experienced Elder Law attorney will be able to answer these questions after examining the documents that you signed and the conditions under which the patient entered the nursing home.

AN ESTATE WITH ASSETS

If the decedent owed money and he died owning property, belonging to him alone, such as a bank account, securities, or real property, then there may be money available to pay monies owed by the decedent. It is up to the decedent's Personal Representative to pay all valid debts, but to do so the Personal Representative first must gain possession of the decedent's assets. To gain possession of the decedent's assets, there will need to be some sort of probate procedure to determine who is entitled to the decedent's property.

Once the probate procedure begins, all of the decedent's creditors will be given an opportunity to come forward and produce evidence showing how much is owed. The Personal Representative needs to look over each unpaid invoice and decide whether it is a valid bill. The problem with making that decision is that the decedent is not here to say whether he actually received the goods and services now being billed to his estate.

That is especially the case for medical or nursing care bills. An example of improper billing brought to the attention of this author was that of a bill submitted for a physical examination of the decedent. The bill listed the date of the examination as July 10th, but the decedent died on July 9th. Other incorrect billings may not be as obvious, so each invoice needs to be carefully examined.

If the Personal Representative decides to challenge a bill, and is unable to settle the matter with the creditor, then the probate court will decide whether the debt is valid and should be paid.

MEDICAL BILLS COVERED BY INSURANCE

If the decedent had health insurance you may receive an invoice stamped "THIS IS NOT A BILL." This means that the health care provider has submitted the bill to the decedent's health insurance company and expects to be paid by them. Even though payment is not requested, it is important that you verify that the bill is valid for two reasons:

➢ **LATER LIABILITY**

If the insurer refuses to pay the claim, the facility will seek payment from whoever is in possession of the decedent's property, and that may reduce the amount inherited by the beneficiaries.

➢ **INCREASED HEALTH CARE COSTS**

Regardless of whether the decedent was covered by a private health care insurer or Medicare, improper billing increases the cost of health insurance to all of us. Consumers pay high premiums for health coverage. We, as taxpayers, all share the cost of Medicare. If unnecessary or fraudulent billing is not checked, then ultimately, we all pay.

 *Special Situation*   MEDICARE FRAUD

If you believe that you have come across a case of Medicare fraud, you can call the ANTI-FRAUD HOTLINE 1-800-447-8477 and report the incident to the Office of the Inspector General of the United States Department of Health and Human Services.

You can also call the ARIZONA AGING AND ADULT ADMINISTRATION in Phoenix, Arizona at (602)542-4446.

HOW TO CHECK MEDICARE BILLING

If the decedent was covered by Medicare, then an important billing question is whether the health care provider agreed to accept Medicare *assignment of benefits*, meaning that they agreed to accept payment directly from Medicare. If so, the maximum liability for the patient is **20%** of the amount determined as reasonable by Medicare. For example, suppose a doctor bills Medicare $1,000 for medical treatment of the decedent. If Medicare determines that a reasonable fee is $800, then the patient is liable for 20% of the $800 ($160).

Health care providers who do not accept Medicare assignment, bill the patient directly. They can charge up to 15% more than the amount allowed by Medicare. If the decedent knew and agreed to be liable for the payment, then his estate may be liable for whatever Medicare doesn't pay. For example, if a doctor's bill is $1,000 and Medicare allows $800, then Medicare will reimburse the decedent's estate 80% of $800 ($640). The doctor may charge the estate 15% more than the $800 ($920) and the estate may be liable for the difference: $920 - $640 or $280.

To summarize:
For health care providers accepting Medicare assignment, the most they can bill the decedent's estate is 20% of what Medicare pays (not 20% of what they bill.)

Those who do not accept Medicare assignment, can bill 15% more than the amount allowed by Medicare. The decedent's estate may be liable for the difference between the amount billed and the amount paid by Medicare.

In either case, if the decedent had secondary health care insurance, then the secondary insurer may be liable for the difference. If you have a question about Medicare billing call MEDICARE PART B CUSTOMER SERVICE: 800-333-7586.

Special Situation ▷ DENIAL OF MEDICARE COVERAGE

If the health care provider reports to you that services provided to the decedent are not covered by Medicare, or if the facility submits the bill to Medicare and Medicare refuses to pay, then check to see if you agree with that ruling by determining what services are covered under Medicare. See page 43 of this book for information about how to obtain pamphlets that explain what medical treatments are covered under Medicare.

If you believe that the decedent has wrongly been denied coverage, then you can appeal that decision. Arizona has eight regional AREA AGENCY ON AGING. This agency assists people with their Medicare appeals. The service is free of charge. Call 800-432-4040 for the telephone number of the AREA AGENCY ON AGING office nearest you.

If there is no office convenient to you, then call the Arizona Bar (602) 340-7300 for a referral to an attorney experienced in Medicare appeals. Some attorneys work *pro bono* (literally for the public good; i.e. without charge) but most charge to assist in an appeal. Federal statute 42 U.S.C. §406(a)(2)(A) limits the amount an attorney may charge for a successful medical appeal to 25% of the amount recovered or $4,000, whichever is the smaller amount.

SOME THINGS ARE CREDITOR PROOF

Sometimes it happens that the decedent had money or property titled in his name only but he also had a significant amount of debt. In such cases the beneficiaries may wonder whether they should go through a probate procedure if there will be little, if anything, left after creditors are paid. Before coming to that conclusion consider that some assets are protected by Arizona statute:

✧ THE HOMESTEAD ALLOWANCE ✧

The surviving spouse is entitled to keep $18,000 that is exempt from the claims of any creditor of the decedent. This sum is called the *homestead allowance*. If there is no surviving spouse, then the decedent's minor or dependent children are entitled to divide the $18,000 between them. A *dependent child* is one who received at least half of his support from the decedent (AZ 14-2402).

✧ FAMILY ALLOWANCE ✧

The spouse and dependent children of the decedent are entitled to a reasonable allowance in money out of the estate for their maintenance while the estate is being probated. This *family allowance* can be paid in a lump sum, or monthly, but the total amount cannot exceed $12,000 without a special order from the court (AZ 14-2405). The family allowance is exempt from the claims of creditors. The only items that can be paid before paying the family allowance are the homestead allowance and the expenses of administration (probate filing fees, publishing notice to creditors, attorney's fees, etc.).

✧ EXEMPT PROPERTY ✧

In addition to the family allowance, the surviving spouse is also entitled to keep any of the following items:
the household furniture
automobiles
furnishings
appliances
personal effects
up to $7,000 in value (not counting monies owed on the property). If the value of these items does not add up to $7,000, then the spouse is entitled to any other asset of the estate to make up the $7,000 value.

If there is no surviving spouse then the decedent's children are entitled to divide the *exempt property* equally between them (AZ 14-2403). In the state of Arizona, an adopted child has the same rights as a natural child, so if any of the decedent's children were adopted, then that child is entitled to an equal share of the exempt property (AZ 14-2114).

✧ THE HOMESTEAD EXEMPTION ✧

Anyone who resides in the state of Arizona is entitled to a homestead exemption in the amount of $100,000 of equity in the property. By *equity* we mean the current value of the property, less monies owed on it. If a person owns their residence, a creditor cannot force the sale of the property unless there is more than $100,000 in equity in the homestead. Of course this exemption does not apply to someone who holds a mortgage on the property or for a labor or construction liens on the property (AZ 33-1103).

Only one homestead exemption may be claimed by a married couple, but if the decedent owned the homestead jointly with his spouse, then that $100,000 homestead exemption now belongs to his spouse (AZ 33-1101). If he was single, then the exemption is lost once he dies.

✧ LIFE INSURANCE PROCEEDS ✧

If the life of the decedent was insured and the beneficiary of the policy was his spouse or his child, then up to $20,000 of the proceeds of the policy are exempt from the claims of the decedent's creditors (Arizona statute 33-1126 A1). The statute also provides that if the decedent was the legal guardian of a child, and had a life insurance policy payable to the child, then up to $20,000 of those funds are protected from the creditors of the decedent.

The statute does not state whether only one $20,000 exemption is allowed. Suppose the decedent left one policy worth $20,000 to his son and another worth $20,000 to his daughter. Are both policies exempt from the claims of his creditors? This author could find no case where a judge ruled, giving an answer. Perhaps the question never came up because life insurance policies generally bypass the probate procedure and are paid directly to the beneficiary.

 EMPLOYMENT INSURANCE PROCEEDS

If the insurance policy was work-related (insured as part of employment), then the policy may be regulated by the federal government under the Employee Retirement Income Security Act ("ERISA"). If there is a question, as to whether the proceeds of a policy can be reached by a creditor, then it is important to consult with an attorney.

✧ FEDERAL RETIREMENT PLANS ✧

Federal retirement plans 401(a), 403 a & b, 408 A, 409, and deferred plans under section 457 of the US Internal Revenue Code are exempt from the claims of creditors. All monies received by beneficiaries of these plans are protected from the decedent's creditors (AZ 33-1126 C).

✧ THERE IS A STATUTE OF LIMITATIONS ✧

Finally, consider that there is a statute of limitations for bringing a claim against the Probate Estate of the decedent. The first job of the Personal Representative is to tell the decedent's creditors that the decedent died, and that a probate procedure is in progress. If the Personal Representative knows the identity of a creditor, then he must give the creditor notice by mail. The Personal Representative must publish notice in the newspaper for three successive weeks to inform any unknown creditor of the death. If a creditor fails to file a claim within four months after the date of the first publication, then his claim is barred (AZ 14-3801).

But what if no one starts a probate procedure? Arizona statute 14-3803 imposes a two year statute of limitations from the date of the decedent's death. If a claim is not filed within two years after the death, then that claim cannot be enforced against the estate, the Personal Representative, or any of the beneficiaries.

There are exceptions to the two-year limit such as mortgages and federal claims and certain liens on the decedent's property. But, in general, if no one starts a probate procedure and two years have passed from the date of the death, then the beneficiaries may be able to obtain possession of the decedent's assets free from creditor claims.

But read the next page before you decide to wait out the two years.

 **LAWYER**

DECEDENT LEAVING CONSIDERABLE DEBT

If the decedent died leaving much debt and no property then the solution is simple. No probate, no one gets paid. But if the decedent had property and died owing a significant amount of money, his heirs may be tempted to wait the two year period and begin probate at that time. Such strategy may turn out to be more hassle than its worth. Some creditors are tenacious and will use whatever legal strategy is available in order to be paid. For example, if no one starts a probate procedure, then once 45 days has passed from the date of death, any creditor can petition the court to be appointed as Personal Representative of the estate (AZ 14-3203).

If a creditor tries to become Personal Representative, then the family may object to the appointment. This may trigger a court battle over who has the right to be appointed as Personal Representative. Once probate begins there could be additional litigation regarding which bills should be paid and in what priority. Court battles are expensive, emotionally as well as financially. Before you decide to wait out a creditor by postponing probate for two years, consult with an attorney experienced in probate matters for his/her opinion about the best way to administer the estate.

MONIES OWED TO THE DECEDENT

Suppose you owed money to the decedent? Do you need to pay that debt now that he is dead? That depends on whether there is some written document that says the debt is forgiven once the decedent dies. For example, suppose the decedent lent you money to buy your home. If he left a Will saying that once he dies, your debt is forgiven, then you do not need to make any more payments. If you signed a mortgage at the time and if that mortgage was recorded, then the Personal Representative of the decedent's estate should sign and record a satisfaction of that mortgage. If you signed a promissory note then the Personal Representative should mark the promissory note "PAID IN FULL" and return the original note to you.

If you owed the decedent money and there is no Will, or if there is a Will and no mention of forgiving the debt, then you still owe the money. You need to continue to make payments. If you borrowed the money from the decedent and his spouse, then you will pay the money to the spouse. If you borrowed the money from the decedent only, then the debt becomes an asset to the estate of the decedent, meaning that you now owe the money to his heirs. If you are one of those heirs, you can deduct the money from your inheritance.

For example, suppose your father left $70,000 in a bank account to be divided equally between you and your two brothers. If you owe your father $20,000, then your father's estate is really worth $90,000. Your share of the inheritance is $30,000. Instead of paying the $20,000, you can agree to receive $10,000 and have the $20,000 debt forgiven. Each of your brothers will then receive their $30,000 in cash.

CHAPTER 5
WHO ARE THE BENEFICIARIES?

A question that comes up early on is who is entitled to the property of the decedent. To answer the question you first need to know how the property was titled (owned) as of the date of death.

There are three ways to own property. The decedent could have owned property jointly with another person; or in trust for another person; or the decedent could have owned property that was titled in his name only.

In general, upon the decedent's death:

Joint Property with rights of survivorship belongs to the surviving joint owner.

Trust Property belongs to the beneficiary of the trust.

Property owned by the **decedent only** belongs to beneficiaries named in the Will.
If there is no Will, then the property is distributed according to the Arizona Law of Intestate Succession.

NOTE ⇨ If the decedent was married, then his spouse may have rights in his property.

This chapter explains each of these types of ownership in detail.

PROPERTY HELD JOINTLY

Bank accounts, securities, motor vehicles, real property can all be owned jointly by two or more people. If one of the joint owners dies, then the survivor(s) continue to own their own share of the property. Who owns the share belonging to the decedent depends on how the joint ownership was set up:

THE JOINT BANK ACCOUNT

If two or more people open a bank account, then it is called a *multiple party* or *joint account*. During their lifetime, each person named on the account, is entitled to as much as they contributed unless there is clear evidence of a different intent. If a husband and wife own the account then it is presumed they each own half of the account (AZ 14-6211).

If two people open an account they must sign a contract of deposit with the bank saying who will get their share of the account should one of them die. If the parties do not want the joint owner of the account to get the other's share, then the contract of deposit with the bank will state:
"At death of party, deceased party's ownership
passes as part of deceased party's estate."
or the contract of deposit will identify the account as a
"tenancy in common."
In these cases, there is no *right of survivorship*, meaning that neither party has the right to the other's share of the account. If one joint owner dies, then his/her share of the account will go the beneficiaries named in the decedent's Will. If there is no Will, then the decedent's share belongs to his heirs under the Laws of Intestate Succession (see page 99).

If there is no right of survivorship, then upon notice of the death, the bank will freeze the account until the beneficiaries of the decedent's share of the account can be established. If a surviving owner withdraws all of the money from the account either just before or after death, then he/she may be liable to the decedent's estate for monies improperly withdrawn.

RIGHT OF SURVIVORSHIP

If a joint account is set up with a right of survivorship, then if one of the owners die, the remaining owners own the account. How much of the account is owned by each surviving owner is determined by Arizona statute 14-6212. If the deceased owner's spouse was a joint owner of the account, then the spouse is entitled to the decedent's share of the account.

EXAMPLE: A husband and wife own a bank account.
         If one dies, the other owns the account 100%.

If the deceased owner was not married to another joint owner of the account, then his share is divided equally between the surviving owners.

EXAMPLE: A husband, wife, and son own a bank account. If the wife dies, the husband owns the wife's share of the account, but if the son dies first, his share will be divided equally between his parents.

A joint account can be set up so that there is a specific beneficiary to the account once they all die. If no beneficiary is named, then once the last owner of the account dies, the funds become part of his estate.

JOINTLY HELD SECURITIES

For securities accounts held jointly, the same rules apply. If the stock or bond is held as jointly with right of survivorship, then upon the death of one owner, the security belongs to the remaining owner. If joint owners hold the security as tenants-in- common, then if one owner dies, his share will go to his heirs and not to the joint owner.

SECURITIES ISSUED IN OTHER STATES

Each state has its own laws regulating securities issued in that state. If the security was issued in another state, then how the account was set up will determine who will inherit the property once the owner dies (AZ 14-6303).

An inspection of the face of the certificate does not always reveal how the security was purchased. For example, if two names are printed on the certificate with no other notation, it could mean that they own the security as tenants-in-common or as joint tenants with rights of survivorship. You will need to contact the company and ask them how the account was set up, and also to send you the necessary forms to either cash in the security or change the certificate to identify the new owner.

BROKERAGE ACCOUNTS

If the decedent held securities in a brokerage account then the name of the owner of that account is printed on the monthly or quarterly brokerage statement. Not all brokerage houses include the name of the joint owner on the brokerage statement so you need to contact the brokerage house and have the broker explain how the account is titled. It may be that the account is held jointly, or perhaps the decedent named a beneficiary who now owns the account. You might wish to request a copy of the contract that is the basis of the account. If you determine that the account is held jointly or for the benefit of someone, then have the brokerage firm forward the necessary forms to make the transfer to the proper owner or beneficiary.

JOINTLY HELD MOTOR VEHICLES

If a motor vehicle is held jointly, the name of each owner is printed on the title to the motor vehicle. Joint ownership is indicated by the words "AND" or "OR" or "AND/OR" for example, the title can read:

HENRY LEE   AND SUSAN PETERS

HENRY LEE   OR SUSAN PETERS

HENRY LEE   AND/OR   SUSAN PETERS

Each of these designations has a different meaning.

AND The word "AND" means that the signature of both parties is needed to transfer title to the motor vehicle. If one of the parties dies, then some sort of probate procedure is necessary to determine who now owns the decedent's half of the car.

OR The word "OR" means that either party can transfer title to the motor vehicle. If one party dies, then the surviving owner can have title transferred to his name alone or to whomever he wishes.

AND/OR The word "AND/OR" has the same legal effect as "OR." The surviving owner is free to transfer title to whomever he wishes.

ARIZONA REAL PROPERTY

The name of the owner of real property is printed on the face of the deed. To determine whether the decedent owned the property jointly with another person, you need to look at the last recorded deed. (See page 53 if you cannot locate the deed.)

Once you have possession of the last recorded deed, look at the person who is named right after the phrase

"... I hereby convey to _____"

or the person named after the phrase

"... I hereby quit claim to _____"

that person is the "GRANTEE." Some deeds refer to the owner of the property as the "PARTY OF THE SECOND PART." The Grantee (or Party of the Second Part) is the owner of the property as of the date of the decedent's death.

DEED HELD AS TENANTS IN COMMON

If the Grantee of a deed identifies the decedent and another as TENANTS IN COMMON then the decedent's share belongs to whomever the decedent named as his beneficiary in his Will. If the decedent died without a Will, then the Arizona Laws of Intestate Succession determine who inherits the property. See page 99 for an explanation of the law.

If property is owned by the decedent as a Tenant In Common, then a probate procedure is necessary. The next chapter describes the type of probate procedure that is necessary in order to establish who is the owner of the decedent's share of the property.

🗐 DEED HELD AS HUSBAND AND WIFE

In many states, a deed held as husband and wife, means that the surviving partner owns the property. This is not the case in Arizona because Arizona is a community property state. In Arizona, it is presumed that a parcel held as husband and wife, is community property with each partner owning half. If a deed identifies the grantee as: TODD AMES and SUSAN AMES, his wife
then if one of them dies, his half of the property will not go to his spouse but to whomever he names in his Will.

If a married couple want the decedent's share to go to the surviving spouse, then the deed needs to say so (AZ 33-431 C). For example, deed can say:
TODD AMES AND SUSAN AMES AS
COMMUNITY PROPERTY WITH RIGHT OF SURVIVORSHIP
- or the deed can read -
TODD AMES AND SUSAN AMES,
NOT AS COMMUNITY PROPERTY
BUT AS JOINT TENANTS WITH RIGHT OF SURVIVORSHIP.

 LAWYER   DIVORCED PRIOR TO DEATH

If the decedent was divorced before he died, and he still holds property together with his ex-spouse, then unless the Final Judgment of Dissolution states otherwise, all property held by the couple as community property or as joint tenancy becomes property held as Tenants-In-Common with each person owning half the property (Az 25-318 B). The decedent's half of the property will descend to his heirs or beneficiaries and not to his former spouse. You will need the assistance of a Probate attorney to have a new deed issued that identifies the new owners of the property.

If the deed identifies the Grantee as the decedent and spouse or another person as JOINT TENANTS WITH RIGHTS OF SURVIVORSHIP then upon the decedent's death, the remaining tenants own the property. If you are the surviving owner, you do not need to do anything to establish that you now own the property, but the decedent's name still remains on the deed. An attorney can draft an Affidavit of Termination of Joint Tenancy Interest for the remaining owner(s) to sign. Once the Affidavit and death certificate are recorded, the decedent's name is, in effect, removed from the deed.

If you later sell the property, the buyer will know that the joint owner is dead and has no interest in the property, but the buyer still wants to be assured that there are no Arizona estate taxes that might become a lien on the property as a result of the decedent's death. The closing could be delayed while the closing agent scrambles to obtains a tax release from the Arizona Department of Revenue. To avoid this problem, you can have your attorney apply for a Waiver of Estate Taxes from the Department of Revenue. When it is received the attorney can have the Waiver recorded along with the death certificate and Affidavit. Once these documents are recorded, you can sell the property without any delay caused by the decedent's death.

Even if you don't intend to sell the property, it is important that you take care of these matters soon after the decedent's death, otherwise you might be leaving a problem for your heirs. They will be need to figure out the decedent's finances so that they can obtain his Waiver from the Arizona Department of Revenue. That could be difficult to do if the decedent died years before your death.

 **JOINT TENANTS BUT NO STATED RIGHTS OF SURVIVORSHIP**

If the deed names two or more people as the Grantee but does not identify whether they are Tenants In Common or Joint Tenants With Rights of Survivorship then according to Arizona Statute 33-431 they hold title as Tenants in Common. There are exceptions to the rule. If an owner of real property transfers the property to himself and someone else without stating whether there are any rights of survivorship, then a joint tenancy with right of survivorship is created. For example, if RICHARD GOMEZ conveys to

RICHARD GOMEZ and his brother JOSE GOMEZ

then should either brother die, the property will belong to the surviving owner. Similarly, if a married couple hold title as community property, they can create a right of survivorship by transferring the property to themselves as husband and wife (AZ 33-431 B, C).

There are other exceptions to the rule, so if there are two or more grantees and the deed does not clearly identify whether they are Tenants-In -Common or Joint Tenants With Rights of Survivorship, then it is important to consult with an experienced probate attorney to determine who owns the property once one of the owners dies.

📄 DEED WITH A LIFE ESTATE

A *Life Estate* interest in real property means that the person who owns the Life Estate has the right to live in that property until he/she dies. While the owner of the Life Estate is alive, the Grantee has no right to occupy the property. Once the owner of the Life Estate dies, the property belongs to the person who is named as Grantee on the deed.

You can identify a Life Estate interest by examining the face of the deed. If somewhere on the face of the deed you see the phrase RESERVING A LIFE ESTATE to the decedent then the Grantee(s) now own the property. For example, suppose the granting paragraph of the deed reads:

THIS INDENTURE, made this day
between PETER REILLY, a single man,
party of the first part,
hereinafter referred to as "Grantor"
and, RACHEL SMITH, a married woman,
party of the second part,
hereinafter referred to as "Grantee"

RESERVING A LIFE ESTATE TO THE GRANTOR

Once Peter dies, all Rachel need do is record the death certificate to establish her ownership of the property. See page 22 for an explanation of how to record the death certificate.

 **OUT OF STATE PROPERTY**

This chapter relates only to property owned by the decedent in the state of Arizona. If the decedent owned property in another state or country, then the laws of that state or country, and perhaps even the laws of Arizona, will determine who inherits the property. You will need to consult with an attorney in that state to determine who owns the property now that the Grantee is dead.

 The above discussion on the different types of ownership of real property presumes that you are in possession of the most recent deed.

The decedent could have signed a different deed after the deed you have in your possession. Before you come to a conclusion about who inherits the property it is advisable to have an attorney, or a title company, do a title search to determine the owner of the property as of the decedent's date of death.

PROPERTY HELD IN TRUST

BANK/ SECURITY ACCOUNTS
If a bank account or security account is registered in the name of the decedent "in trust for" or "for the benefit of" someone, then once the bank has a certified copy of the death certificate, the bank will turn over the money in that account to the beneficiary.

THE PAY ON DEATH ACCOUNT
If the decedent set up a PAY ON DEATH ("POD") account, or if the account is "for the benefit of" or "in trust for" then once the owner of the account dies, the bank will give the funds in the account to the beneficiary named in the contract of deposit. If two or more beneficiaries are named, then each will receive an equal share. If one of the beneficiaries dies before the owner of the account, then the remaining beneficiaries will share the money. If no beneficiary survives, then the money goes to the decedent's estate.
EXAMPLE: A father sets up a POD account for his daughter. If the daughter dies first and her father does not name a new beneficiary, then the money will be distributed as part of his estate.

The same principal applies if the decedent owned an account jointly with someone, the only difference being that no monies are given to the beneficiaries until both joint owners are deceased (AZ 14-6212 B2).
EXAMPLE: A husband and wife set up a POD account for the benefit of their 3 children. If one of the children dies before his parents, then the remaining children will share the account once both parents are gone.

As explained above, if the owner of bank account dies, then who owns the account depends on the way the account was set up with the bank. You will need to obtain a copy of the contract of deposit to determine who has the right to the account. If you cannot find a copy of the contract among the decedent's records, then you can call the bank and ask them for a copy.

TRANSFER ON DEATH REGISTRATION
As with bank accounts, joint owners of a security can direct the company to give the security to a beneficiary when all of the owners of the security are deceased. In such cases the face of the security might have a "transfer on death" ("TOD") or "pay on death" ("POD") notation:

ROBERT SMITH AND ANN SMITH, HIS WIFE **TOD** LEE SMITH

As with the POD account, if Ann dies, then Robert is the sole owner of the security. He is free to sell it or keep it as he sees fit. Lee has no right to the security until Robert is also deceased (Arizona statute 14-6306). If Lee dies before Robert, then the security will become part of Robert's estate to be distributed to the beneficiaries named in his Will. If Robert dies without a Will, then the TOD account is distributed according to Arizona's Law of Intestate Succession (Arizona statue 14-6307).

If the bank or security account is registered in the name of the decedent "as trustee," that means the decedent was the trustee of a trust and the bank will turn over that account to the Successor Trustee of the trust. Banks usually require a copy of the trust when the account was opened, so the bank probably knows the identity of the Successor Trustee. If the trust was amended to name a different Successor Trustee, you need to present the bank with a copy of that amendment together with a certified copy of the death certificate.

MOTOR VEHICLE

If the motor vehicle is held in the name of the decedent "as trustee," then the motor vehicle is part of the trust property. The motor vehicle remains in the trust once the decedent trustee dies. The Successor Trustee will need to contact the motor vehicle bureau to have title changed to that of the Successor Trustee.

REAL PROPERTY

If the decedent had a trust and put property that he owned in the trust then the deed may read something like this:

THIS INDENTURE
made this day between
JOHN ZAMORA and MARIA ZAMORA,
his wife, party of the first part,
hereinafter referred to as "Grantor"
and JOHN ZAMORA **trustee of the**
JOHN ZAMORA TRUST AGREEMENT
DATED FEBRUARY 26, 1999,
party of the second part,
hereinafter referred to as "Grantee"

Once the trustee (John Zamora) dies then that property remains in the trust. The trust document will say whether the person who takes John's place as trustee (the *Successor Trustee*) should sell or keep the property or perhaps give it to a beneficiary. If no instruction is given, then what the Successor Trustee does with the property may be affected by laws relating to the administration of trust property in the state where the property is located. If you are a beneficiary of the trust and you are concerned about what the Successor Trustee will do with the property, then it is best to consult with your attorney.

PROPERTY IN DECEDENT'S NAME ONLY

If the decedent owned property that was in his name only (not jointly or in trust for someone) then that property is identified as the decedent's **Probate Estate**. It is called the Probate Estate because some sort of probate procedure will be necessary before the heirs can get possession of that property. Who is entitled to the decedent's Probate Estate depends on whether the decedent died *testate* (with a Will) or *intestate* (without a Will).

If the decedent died testate, then the Will states who is to receive the property. If a person neglects to write a Will then the state provides one for him in the form of the Laws of Intestate Succession. Arizona is a community property state so if the decedent was a resident of Arizona and he was married, then the Arizona Law of Intestate Succession applies to the decedent's separate property and his half of the community property.

Arizona's Law of Intestate Succession recognizes the right of the family to inherit the decedent's property. The law covers all possible relationships beginning with the decedent's spouse. The term "spouse" means someone who was legally married to the decedent in the state of Arizona or elsewhere. It does not include common law marriages (AZ 25-111). It does not include same sex marriages, nor incestuous marriages (AZ 25-101). In Arizona, a marriage between first cousins is considered to be incestuous unless both were over the age of 65 when married and a Superior Court judge approved the union after receiving proof that at least one of the cousins was unable to reproduce (AZ 25-101 B).

ARIZONA'S INTESTATE LAW

Arizona's Law of Intestate Succession covers all possible relationships:

MARRIED

If the decedent was married and had no surviving *descendants* (children, grandchildren, great-grandchildren, etc.) or if all of the decedent's children are also those of the surviving spouse, then all of the intestate estate goes to the surviving spouse (AZ 14-2102 (1)).

In Arizona, an adopted child has the same rights as does a natural child of the descendant. A child born out of wedlock is a lineal descendant of the father with the same rights as those children born during marriage. If the father did not acknowledge his paternity of a child, then it will take a court order to establish that the child is his/her father's lineal descendant (AZ 14-2114).

MARRIED WITH SEPARATE CHILDREN

If the decedent was married and not all of the decedent's children are those of the surviving spouse, then the spouse inherits half of the decedent's separate property and the children inherit the other half.

If the decedent owned community property with his spouse, then his spouse keeps her share of the community property and decedent's share goes to his children. (AZ 14-2102 (2)).

SINGLE WITH CHILDREN

If the decedent was not married when he died, but he had descendants, then they inherit all of his property *by representation*. Arizona statute 14-2709 (A) defines the term "by representation" as follows:

If an applicable statute or a governing instrument calls for property to be distributed **by representation** or **per capita at each generation**, the property is divided into as many equal shares as there are surviving descendants in the generation nearest to the designated ancestor that contains one or more surviving descendants and deceased descendants in the same generation who left any surviving descendants. Each surviving descendant in the nearest generation is allocated one share. Any remaining shares are combined and then divided in the same manner among the surviving descendants of the deceased descendants as if the surviving descendants who were allocated a share and their surviving descendants had predeceased the distribution date.

If you understood the above definition and you are not a lawyer, then you missed your calling. For the rest of us (even lawyers) its a head-scratcher. Perhaps the best way to explain the term is by example:

ALL CHILDREN SURVIVE

Suppose the decedent was unmarried with 4 children, Ann, Barry, Carl, David and he dies intestate, then each of his children get 25% of his estate.

CHILD WITHOUT DESCENDANTS DIES BEFORE DECEDENT

If Ann dies before her father leaving no descendants, then Barry, Carl and David divide the estate between them and each gets one third.

CHILDREN WITH DESCENDANTS DIES BEFORE DECEDENT

Suppose instead that only Carl and David survived their father. If Ann died leaving 2 children and Barry died leaving 3 children, then the estate is divided into 4 shares — one for each surviving child and one share for each deceased child who left descendants.

Carl and David each get their 25% share. The other 50% of the estate is divided equally among the five grandchildren; i.e., each will get $1/10^{th}$ of the intestate estate.

SINGLE, NO CHILDREN

If the decedent was single and had no children, then the property goes to his parents equally. If only one of his parents is alive, then all of the property goes to that parent (AZ 14-2103 (2)). If it happened that a parent did not treat a child as his own, and refused to support the child, then that parent loses his right to inherit the child's property (AZ 14-2114 C).

SINGLE, NO CHILD, NO PARENT

If the decedent had no surviving descendant or parent, then the intestate estate goes to the descendants of his parents. This includes all of the decedent's brothers and sisters and the children of a deceased sibling; i.e, the decedent's nieces and nephews. The property is distributed "by representation at each generation." (AZ 14-2103 (3))

A relative who is related by half blood inherits the same as one who is related by whole blood (AZ 14-2107). For example, if the decedent had a brother with the same parent and two sisters with the same father but a different mother, then all three siblings inherit an equal share of the decedent's estate.

SINGLE, NO CHILD, NO PARENT, NO SIBLING

If the decedent had none of the above, then the estate goes to the decedent's grandparents. If none of his grandparents survives him then the intestate estate goes to the descendants of the grandparents. This includes all of the decedent's aunts, uncles, and children of a deceased aunt or uncle, i.e., the decedent's cousins As before, distribution is by representation at each generation (AZ 14-2103 (4)).

THE STATE: HEIR OF LAST RESORT

If a person dies without a Will and he has absolutely no surviving relatives, then the intestate estate goes to the state of Arizona. (AZ 14-2105)

NO SHARE FOR KILLER

If an heir is convicted of killing the decedent, then that heir forfeits all benefits with respect to the decedent's estate. In such case, regardless of whether the decedent died with or without a will, his estate is distributed as if the killer died before the decedent (AZ 14-2803).

WHO DIED FIRST?

Arizona statute 14-2104 requires that a beneficiary must survive the decedent by at least 120 hours for purposes of intestate succession; however this rule does not apply if an imposition of the 120 hour limit would result in the state taking the decedent's property.

The same 120 hour rule for intestate succession applies to owners of joint property. To avoid the problem of trying to determine who survived the other in the case of simultaneous death, Arizona statute 14-2702 requires that the joint owner or beneficiary of property located in Arizona live at least 120 hours (5 days) more than the decedent. If a beneficiary dies within 5 days of the decedent then the property is distributed as if the beneficiary had died first.

If both joint owners of an account die within 5 days of each other, then half of the account is distributed as if that party were the survivor. For example, if two brothers, Frank and Neil, own a joint bank account and they die in the same automobile accident, then Frank's half of the account gets distributed as if Neil died first, and Neil's half gets distributed as if Frank died first.

WHEN TO CHALLENGE A WILL

If the decedent left a Will, then the Will states who is to receive the property. Most Wills are short and easy to read, however, you may come across an unfamiliar legal term such as the term *per stirpes*, for example:

"I leave the rest, residue and remainder of my property to my children, Ann, Barry and Carl, in equal shares, per stirpes."

This means that if one child dies before the decedent, then the share intended for that child is to be divided equally among the lineal descendants of that child.

The decedent may have left a Will that he wrote in his own hand, but no one witnessed him signing the Will. Such a Will is called a *holographic Will.* The state of Arizona recognizes such a Will as being valid, providing the signature and the main parts of the Will are in the handwriting of the decedent (AZ 14-2503).

Not all states will accept a holographic Will into probate. If the decedent died in Arizona but his primary residence was in another state, the probate court of that state might decide that there is no valid Will and that the decedent died intestate. In such a case, the Laws of Intestate Succession of that state will determine who inherits the decedent's property.

The problem with a holographic Will, in this or any other state, is its authenticity. Because no one saw the decedent sign the Will, it is hard to determine whether the Will was written by the decedent or is a forgery. If all the decedent left was a holographic Will, then you should consult with an attorney experienced in Probate matters.

THE VALID WILL

In the state of Arizona a Will is valid if at the time the decedent made the Will:

➤ he was 18 years of age or older

➤ he was not being unduly influenced by anyone

➤ he signed the Will in the presence of at least two witnesses

➤ he was of sound mind meaning, he knew what he was doing (namely making a Will); what property he had, and who of his relatives would, under ordinary circumstances, expect to inherit his property.

If a Will is valid in the state of Arizona, then the probate court makes every effort to carry out the intent of the decedent, unless the Will is contrary to the laws of the state. One such example is that of Sylvia. Hers was not an easy life. She worked long hours as a waitress. She divorced her hard-drinking first husband. The final judgment gave her cash and securities worth $30,000, and sole custody of their son, Richard. After the divorce Sylvia had her attorney prepare a Will leaving all she owned to Richard.

Some years later Sylvia met and married Harry, a chef at the restaurant where she worked. Sylvia continued to work, even after the birth of their twin girls. She kept the securities and money she owned in a separate account. The only money she took from the account was to pay for a new car that she purchased for herself.

Richard was 19, and his stepsisters 12, when Sylvia died after a lengthy battle with cancer. Before she died, she told her son, Richard, that she had not changed her Will because she wanted him to have all she owned. She said Harry had a good job and she was sure he would take good care of his daughters.

She never discussed her Will with Harry, so he was surprised, and angry, when he learned that she wanted everything she had to go to Richard. He complained to his attorney: "I took good care of her all these years, and yet she didn't even consider leaving something to me or our daughters. She always favored Richard over the girls. It just isn't right."

The lawyer explained Arizona law:
"Your wife wrote her Will before she married you. Under Arizona statute 14-2301, you have no right to challenge the Will because she gave her property to her son. But your daughters are entitled to share equally in property given to Richard. Under Arizona statute 14-2302, any child who is born after the decedent executed the Will is entitled to a share of the estate unless the decedent gave all of her property to the parent of the omitted child. In this case Sylvia gave all of her property to Richard and not to you, so the girls are entitled to an equal share of Sylvia's estate.

Although you have no grounds to challenge Sylvia's Will on your own behalf, you are still entitled to receive your Homestead Allowance of $18,000; and you are entitled to Sylvia's car as part of the $7,000 Exempt Property that you are allowed to keep. Either before or after marriage, a person can waive (give up) his rights in the Homestead Allowance and Exempt property (AZ 14-2207). If you did not sign any agreement waiving these rights then you have the right to the car and the $18,000 at this time.

We could argue that the girls are entitled to a Family Allowance because Sylvia contributed to their support up till the time she became too ill to work. I see no point in doing so because Arizona statute 14-2404 makes any amount the girls receive as a Family Allowance to be set off against the amount they receive as a beneficiary of the Will."

You may think that Richard received some small amount from his mother's estate — at least his one third share of the cash and securities. Not so. Harry refused to contribute anything toward the cost of Sylvia's funeral so that bill had to be paid from the money she left. By the time the Homestead Allowance, funeral expenses, medical bills, and the cost of probating the estate were paid, there was virtually nothing left for him.

Had Sylvia known about Arizona law, she could have transferred her securities, cash and car to her son before she died. She was free to do so when she was alive because these items belonged to her as separate property.

But the moral of the story, for the purpose of this discussion, is that if you believe that the decedent's Will is not valid or is not drafted according to Arizona law, then you need to consult with an attorney experienced in Probate matters to determine your legal rights under that Will.

CHAPTER 6
GETTING POSSESSION OF THE PROPERTY

Knowing who is entitled to receive the decedent's property is one thing. Getting that property is another. As explained in the previous chapter if the property is held jointly with someone, or in a trust for someone, then the property belongs to the joint owner or beneficiary. The joint owner or beneficiary is free to take possession of the property, with the understanding that if money is needed to pay the decedent's debts, then the owner or beneficiary must be prepared to return the money to the decedent's estate (see page 69).

If the decedent held property in his name only, then some sort of probate procedure is necessary in order to transfer ownership to the proper beneficiary. Many of the probate procedures allowed by Arizona statute are relatively simple and can be done without the assistance of an attorney. The counsel of an attorney, who is experienced in probate matters, is recommended for those estates that exceed $50,000 in personal property; or that exceed $50,000 in real property; or in cases where there is some contest — perhaps whether a valid Will exists, or whether a creditor has the right to be paid.

This chapter explains the various probate procedures and when it is appropriate to use that procedure.

DISTRIBUTING THE PERSONAL EFFECTS

Too often, the first person to discover the body will help himself to the decedent's *personal effects* (clothing, jewelry, appliances, electrical equipment, cameras, books, household items and furnishing, etc.). Unless that person is the decedent's sole beneficiary, such action is unconscionable, if not illegal.

If the decedent was married and did not have children, then all of the decedent's personal effects belong to his spouse. Even if the decedent had children, the spouse is entitled to all of the household furnishings and appliances up to $7,000 in value (see page 77). If the decedent was not married, then all of his personal effects should be given to the Personal Representative named in the decedent's Will. The Personal Representative then has the duty to distribute the property according to Arizona law or as directed in the Will.

If there is no Will, then the next of kin need to determine whether the decedent left a list or written statement of how he wanted his personal property distributed. Arizona statute 14-2513 states that a person may make gifts of tangible personal property by means of a written statement or list prepared either before or after the person signs a Will. If the decedent left a written statement of how he wanted his personal effects distributed, then those wishes need to be respected.

If the decedent did not have a Will, and was not married, then his children are entitled to divide all of the personal effects among themselves in approximately equal proportions. If the decedent was single and without children then the personal effects of the decedent are distributed according to Arizona's Laws of Intestate Succession. See Chapter 5 for an explanation of the law.

Most personal effects have little, if any, monetary value. The property may be worth less than it costs to ship. In such case, the beneficiaries may decide to donate the personal effects to the decedent's favorite charity. If the decedent happened to own some item of great value such as an antique or an expensive painting then a formal probate procedure may be necessary before the asset can be distributed to the proper beneficiary.

WHAT'S EQUAL?

The decedent's Will or if no Will, then the Arizona Law Of Intestate Succession may direct that the decedent's personal property be divided equally between two or more beneficiaries. The problem with the term "equal" is that people have different ideas of what "equal" means. Unless there is clear evidence that the decedent's Will meant something else, "equal" refers to the monetary value of the item and not to the number of items received. For example, to divide the decedent's personal effects equally, one beneficiary may receive an expensive item of jewelry and another beneficiary may receive several items whose overall value is approximately equal to that single piece of jewelry.

When distributing personal effects there needs to be cooperation and perhaps compromise, or else bitter arguments might arise over items of little monetary value. One such argument occurred when an elderly woman died who was rich only in her love for her five children and 12 grandchildren. After the funeral, the children gathered in their mother's apartment. Each child had his/her own furnishings and no need for anything in the apartment. They agreed to donate all of their mother's personal effects to a local charity with the exception of a few items of sentimental value.

Each child took some small item as a remembrance — a handkerchief, a large platter that their mother used to serve family dinners, a doily their mother crocheted. Things went smoothly until it came to her photograph album. Frank, the youngest sibling, said, "I'll take this." Marie objected saying, "But there are pictures in that album that I want." Frank retorted, "You already took all the pictures Mom had on her dresser."

The argument went downhill from there. Unsettled sibling rivalries boiled over, fueled by the hurt of the loss that they were all experiencing. It almost came to blows when the eldest settled the argument: "Frank you make copies of all of the photos in the album for Marie. Marie, you make copies of all of the pictures that you took and give them to Frank. This way you both will have a complete set of Mom's pictures. And while you're at it make copies for the rest of us."

TRANSFERRING SECURITIES

If the value of the decedent's personal property is $50,000, or less, then the beneficiary can get possession of the decedent's securites (stock, bond, CD, bank account) by giving the bank or financial institution an Affidavit. An *affidavit* is a written statement of facts. The *affiant* (the person making the statement) must sign the affidavit in the presence of a notary public and take an oath or affirm that the facts, as written, are true. The Affidavit must be prepared in accordance with Arizona statute 14-3971(B). The statute requires that all the following are true:

30 DAYS PASSED
At least 30 days have passed since the decedent's death.

NO PENDING PROBATE PROCEDURE
No one has petitioned to become Personal Representative or if a Personal Representative has been appointed, then at least one year has passed since he filed a closing statement with the court.

AFFIANT IS THE SUCCESSOR TO THE PROPERTY
The Affiant must be entitled to the property either because the decedent left the property to him by Will or because he inherits the property through intestate succession.

DECEDENT'S PERSONAL PROPERTY IS $50,000 OR LESS
The decedent's personal property is everything he owns in this state or elsewhere, not including any real property that he may own. The value of his personal property as of his date of death, less any money he might own on his personal property, cannot exceed $50,000.

See the next page for a sample affidavit that a beneficiary can use to get possession of his inheritance.

AFFIDAVIT FOR COLLECTION OF PERSONAL PROPERTY

STATE OF ARIZONA   )
County of _____)
_____ being first duly sworn, upon oath,
deposes and says:

1.   _____died on_____ (date) in the county
of _____ state of _____more than 30 days
prior to the execution of this Affidavit.

2. Check either 2a or 2b:

☐   2a. Affiant is the successor of the decedent, entitled to the decedent's property by Will or intestate succession and the value of all of the personal property in the decedent's estate, wherever located, less liens and encumbrances, does not exceed $50,000.

☐ 2b. Affiant is claiming as the ☐ surviving spouse
☐ dependent child of the decedent and the value of all of the personal property in the decedent's estate, wherever located, less liens and encumbrances, does not exceed the greater of $50,000 or the total sums permitted as the allowance in lieu of homestead, exempt property, and the family allowance pursuant to Arizona Revised Statutes, in effect on the date of the decedent's death.

3.   No application or petition for the appointment of a personal representative is pending or has been granted in any jurisdiction.

4.   Decedent owned the following personal property:

ITEM	VALUE OF PROPERTY

5.   Affiant is entitled to receive payment of any debt due the decedent and to receive decedent's tangible personal property or an instrument evidencing the transfer to affiant of any debt, obligation, stock, or chose in action belonging to the decent.

This affidavit is made pursuant to Arizona Revised Statutes 14-3971, as amended, for the purpose of making claim to property of the above named decedent under said statute.

Affiant Name _____
Affiant Signature _____ date_____
Subscribed and sworn to before me this date _____

_____
Notary Public
Seal

SPOUSE — GETTING THE LAST PAYCHECK

The decedent's spouse can use an Affidavit to collect the decedent's last pay check, provided the check is not greater than $5,000 (AZ 14-3971A). The spouse does not need to wait any period of time and can submit the affidavit to the employer whenever it is convenient. The following is a sample affidavit:

NON-PROBATE AFFIDAVIT
I, being first duly sworn, on oath, deposes and says:

1.   The decedent _____
died on_____ (date) at the county of _____
state of _____.

2.   Affiant is the surviving spouse of the decedent and is entitled to receive from the decedent's employer, any wages, salary or other compensation due to the decedent, not in excess of $5,000.

3.   An application or petition for the appointment of a personal representative is not pending or has not been granted in any jurisdiction, or if granted, the personal representative has been discharged or more than one year has elapsed since a closing statement has been filed.

This affidavit is made pursuant to Section 14-3971 (A), Arizona Revised Statutes, as amended, for the purpose of making claim decedent's wages, salary or compensation under said statute.

Affiant Name _____
Affiant Signature _____ date_____

Subscribed and sworn to before me this date _____
at _____ County, state of _____

_____
Notary Signature and Seal

IRS REFUNDS OF $500 OR LESS

As explained in Chapter 2, you need to file the decedent's final income tax return (IRS form 1040) during the tax season following the date of death. If there is a refund due to the decedent and you are entitled to that money as the beneficiary of the decedent, then you can obtain the refund by filing IRS form 1310 along with the 1040. You can obtain this form 1310 from the decedent's accountant, or if he did not have an accountant and you wish to file yourself, then call the IRS at **1-800-829-3676** to obtain the proper form.

 ## IRS WEB SITE

You can obtain forms, instructions, and publications from the INTERNAL REVENUE SERVICE at the following web sites: IRS FORMS AND INSTRUCTIONS
http://www.irs.ustreas.gov/prod/forms_pubs/forms.html
IRS PUBLICATIONS
http://www.irs.ustreas.gov/prod/forms_pubs/pubs.html

If are appointed as Personal Representative as part of a probate procedure, then you do not need to file form 1310 because once you file the decedent's final income tax return, any refund will be forwarded to you as Personal Representative. Similarly, a surviving spouse does not need to file form 1310 because the spouse will automatically receive any refund due on that return.

STATE INCOME TAX REFUND

If you are the spouse of the decedent or if you have been appointed as Personal Representative, then you need to file the final state income tax return at the same time you file the federal income tax return. If there is a refund then you will need to complete Arizona form 131:

Claim For Refund on Behalf of Deceased Taxpayer

See page 58 for an explanation of how to obtain this form.

DEPOSITING THE CHECK

If the refund check sent to you from the IRS or the state is in the name of the decedent and you have a joint account with the decedent, then you can print on the back of the check: FOR **DEPOSIT ONLY** followed by the account number, and then deposit the check to that account.

If the refund check is in the name of the decedent and there is no joint account, then to obtain possession of the funds you can use the same affidavit as previously described on page 112.

TRANSFERRING THE CAR

If the decedent owned a motor vehicle then it needs to be re-titled into the name of the beneficiary of the car. You may want to limit the use of the car until it is transferred to the beneficiary. If the decedent's car is involved in an accident before the car is transferred to the new owner, then the decedent's estate will be liable for the damage. Having adequate insurance on the car may save the estate from monetary loss, but a pending lawsuit could delay the probate procedure and prevent any money from being distributed to the beneficiaries until the lawsuit is settled.

Arizona statute 28-4009 requires that the owner of a motor vehicle be insured for at least $30,000 bodily injury and $10,000 property damage. Before making the transfer, have the new owner show proof of insurance. Once the transfer is made, contact the decedent's insurance company and arrange to have the decedent's motor vehicle policy cancelled. The company should refund any unused premium to the estate of the decedent.

WHO IS ENTITLED TO THE MOTOR VEHICLE

As explained in chapter 5, if the decedent held the car jointly with another and title to the car reads "AND/OR" or "OR," then the joint owner now owns the car. The surviving owner should contact the Motor Vehicle Division and remove the decedent's name from the title.

If the decedent owned the car with another and the title reads "AND," then the decedent's half goes to whomever he named in his Will. If he died intestate, then his half goes to his next of kin as determined in the Arizona Law of Intestate Succession (see page 99). A new title will need to be issued identifying the new owner of the car.

If the decedent owned the car in his name only and he used it for his or his family's personal use then, as explained previously, the car goes to his spouse and if there is no spouse, then to the decedent's children.

If the decedent was not survived by a spouse or by a child, then the decedent was free to leave his car to whomever he wished. If the decedent did not make a specific gift of the car in his Will then the car goes to the *residuary beneficiaries* under his Will, i.e. to those people who inherit whatever is left after the decedent's bills and costs of probate are paid. If the decedent did not have a Will, then the car belongs to the decedent's heirs as determined by the Arizona Law of Intestate Succession.

MORE THAN ONE BENEFICIARY

If there is more than one person who has the right to inherit the car, then the beneficiaries need to decide who will take title to the car. The person who takes title to the car may need to compensate the other heirs for their share of the car. If so, then they all need to come to an agreement as to the value of the car.

DETERMINING THE VALUE OF THE CAR

Cars are valued in many different ways. The *collateral* value of the car is the value that banks use to evaluate the car for purposes of making a loan to the owner of the car. Because banks print these values in book form, the collateral value is also referred to as the *book value* of the car. If you were to trade in a car for the purpose of purchasing a new car, then the car dealer will offer you the *wholesale* value of the car. Were you to purchase that same car from a car dealer, then he will price it at its *retail* or *fair market value*. Usually the retail price is highest, wholesale is lowest and the book value of the car is somewhere in between.

You can call your local bank to get the book value of the car. It may be more difficult to obtain the wholesale value of the car because the amount of money a dealer is willing to pay for the car depends on the value of the new car that you are purchasing. You can get some idea of the car's retail value by looking at comparable used car advertisements in the local newspaper.

 You can determine both wholesale and retail values of the car by using one or more of the search engines on the Internet to find web sites that will give both wholesale and retail car values.

LOCATE THE CERTIFICATE OF TITLE

To make the transfer you will need to turn in the certificate of title to the Motor Vehicle Division, together with a certified copy of the death certificate. If you cannot find the certificate of title then contact the Motor Vehicle Division to replace the lost certificate:

Phoenix (602) 255-0072   Tucson (520) 629-9808
Elsewhere in Arizona (800) 324-5425
TDD Service: (800) 324-5425

Once you obtain a copy of the certificate, you may discover that the title identifies a lienholder (lender). In such case, you need to contact the lender to obtain a copy of the promissory note and record of payments. You will not be able to transfer title to the car unless the lender gives written permission to do so. The lender will probably require payment in full before allowing the transfer. Some lenders will allow the beneficiary to take title to the car provided the beneficiary agrees to be responsible for the balance of payments.

If the decedent's car was leased, then the car belongs to the lessor and the lessor has possession of the title certificate. Ask the lessor to give you a copy of the leasing contract. Once you have the contract, you can check to see whether the decedent took out life insurance as part of the agreement. If so, then upon his death the lease is paid in full. The next of kin or the Personal Representative can send the death certificate to the leasing company with a copy of the contract and a letter requesting that the paid contract be transferred to the beneficiary who can use the car for the remainder of the leasing period, or take title to the car, whichever option is available under the lease agreement.

If there is no insurance to pay off the lease, the personal representative (or next of kin) needs to see to it that the person who will inherit the decedent's estate agrees to be liable for the remaining payments. If it happens that the remaining payments exceed the current market value of the car, there may be a temptation to hand the keys over to the leasing company. This may not be the best strategy. The thing to keep in mind is that the leasing contract is a liability to the decedent's estate and the leasing company is now a creditor of the estate.

If the decedent had no assets or if the only assets he had are creditor proof, then simply returning the car may be an option. But if the decedent's estate has assets available to pay the balance of the lease payments, then payments must be continued. If lease payments are not kept current, the lessor has the right to repossess the car AND sue the decedent's estate for the balance of the payments.

Arizona statute 14-3971 (D) provides for the transfer of a motor vehicle on presentation of an affidavit. The Motor Vehicle Division will give you the affidavit (Motor Vehicle Division form 32-6901 RO7/98) at the same time they give you the Title and Registration application form.   To make the transfer by affidavit, the same rules apply as with the transfer of securities, namely:

✧ At least 30 days have passed since death of decedent

✧ Decedent's personal property does not exceed $50,000

✧ No appointment of Personal Representative, or at least one year has passed since closing statement filed

✧ Affiant is the proper successor to the motor vehicle.

TRANSFERRING THE MOBILE HOME

A mobile home is a motor vehicle, so the same affidavit can also be used to transfer the decedent's mobile home. Before transferring the motor vehicle, you need to determine whether the land on which the mobile home is located was leased or owned by the decedent.

If the decedent was renting space in a trailer park, then you need to contact the trailer park owner to transfer the lease to the beneficiary of the mobile home. If the decedent owned the land under the mobile home, then a probate procedure will be necessary to transfer the land to the proper beneficiary. See page 120 for an explanation of how to transfer real property.

NOTIFY THE MOTOR VEHICLE DIVISION OF THE TRANSFER

Once you have transferred the motor vehicle, or if you have terminated the decedent's lease, it is important to notify the Motor Vehicle Division of the transfer so that the decedent's estate will no longer be liable for tickets or accidents. The Personal Representative or next of kin can do so by writing to:

Mail Drop 555M
Motor Vehicle Division
P.O. Box 2100
Phoenix AZ 85001

and notifying them of the name of the new owner, his/her name and address, the Decedent's name, and the date the vehicle was transferred.

TRANSFERRING REAL PROPERTY

To transfer real property owned by the decedent some document needs to be recorded that identities the beneficiary and new owner of the property. If there is going to be a full probate procedure, then the Personal Representative will transfer the decedent's real property to the proper beneficiary. If the decedent's estate is only worth 50,000 or less, then the beneficiary can get possession of the decedent's real property by signing an Affidavit prepared according to Arizona statute. The requirements for transferring real property by Affidavit are similar to those required to transfer personal property:

AT LEAST 6 MONTHS SINCE DATE OF DEATH
A transfer of real property by means of affidavit cannot be made sooner than six months from the date of the decedent's death.

PROPERTY NOT MORE THAN $50,000
The value of the decedent's interest in property owned in the state of Arizona cannot be greater than $50,000. The value is computed by taking the amount shown on the assessment rolls for the year in which the decedent died, less any monies owed on that property. For example, suppose the decedent and his brother owned a condominum as tenants-in-common, with each owning half of the property. If the assessed value of the property is $120,000 and there is a mortgage of $50,000 on the property, then the brothers have $70,000 equity in the property. The decedent's share is worth $35,000. If this is the case then whoever inherits the decedent's share can get title to the property by filing an affidavit with the court.

NO PENDING PROBATE PROCEDURE

No one has petitioned to become Personal Representative or if a Personal Representative has been appointed, then at least one year has passed since he filed a closing statement with the court.

NO ESTATE TAXES DUE

There is no federal or Arizona estate tax due on the decedent's estate.

ALL UNSECURED DEBTS PAID

The funeral expenses, and expenses of the decedent's last illness have been paid. All the decedent's *unsecured* debts have been paid. If the decedent has a mortgage on his home, then that is a *secured* debt. A chattel mortgage on a car is also a secured debt. The creditor of a secured debt is assured of the payment of the debt or the creditor can take possession of the property. An unsecured creditor has no safety net, so Arizona law does not allow the decedent's property to be given to a beneficiary until all unsecured creditors are paid.

AFFIANT IS ENTITLED TO THE PROPERTY

The person who signs the affidavit must be entitled to the property for any one of the following reasons:

➤ Affiant is the heir of the property according to the Arizona Law of Intestate Succession.

➤ Affiant is taking the property instead of taking exempt property or a homestead or family allowance

➤ The decedent named the Affiant as the beneficiary of the property in his last Will

NO ONE ELSE IS ENTITLED TO THE PROPERTY

The decedent was the rightful owner of the property and no one other than Affiant has a right to the property. (AZ 14-3971(E))

If all of these statements are true, then the property, can be transferred by means of an Affidavit. For the transfer to be effective, it will need to be recorded in the county in which the property is located. The County Recorder will not record the Affidavit unless the Probate court approves the transfer and issues a certified copy of the Affidavit. Bottom line — you need to go through a Probate procedure.

If you know your way around the courthouse or if you are an enthusiastic "do it yourselfer," you may want to try to navigate the probate procedure on your own. Your first stop will be the Superior Court in the county where the decedent had his residence. If the decedent was not a resident of Arizona, then you will go to the Superior Court in the county where the property is located.

There is a section within the courthouse called the Quick Court. You can pick up the proper Affidavit form from the Registrar of the court. You will need to pay a filing fee, so you may wish to first call and ask how much you will pay and what documents you need to bring with you.

Once the Affidavit is approved by the court, the Clerk of the Court will issue a certified copy of the Affidavit. You will need to take the certified copy to the office of the Recorder in the county in which the property is located.

As you can see this is a fairly involved procedure. If you make a mistake you might need to employ an attorney to fix the problem. This might cost you more money than if you had employed an attorney in the first place.

You might save yourself much time and maybe even money, if you consult with an attorney before trying to get possession of real property by means of Affidavit.

PROBATING THE SMALL ESTATE

The Affidavit is a good vehicle to use if all that needs to be done is to transfer a few items and the decedent's estate does not exceed $50,000 in either personal or real property. But sometimes it happens that the decedent has a small estate and there is much that needs to be done:

TAX RETURNS FILED
A final tax return needs to be filed and perhaps a tax refund given to the proper beneficiary.

NOTICE
Many different people, including creditors may need to be notified of the death.

BILLS PAID
Bills may need to be paid to many different creditors (telephone bills, credit cards, medical bills, rent payments, car lease payments, etc.)

PROPERTY DISTRIBUTED
Property may need to be distributed to several different beneficiaries after all the bills are paid.

The decedent's spouse may take care of these things without the need for probate, but if the decedent was single, a Personal Representative may need to be appointed to settle the estate. Still another reason to probate the decedent's estate is to start the Statute of Limitations clock ticking. If the Personal Representative notifies a creditor, in writing, of the death, and the creditor does not present his claim within 60 days after the mailing, or 4 months after the Personal Representative publishes notice (whichever is later), then the creditor's claim is forever barred (AZ 14-3801).

SUMMARY ADMINISTRATION

Arizona statute 14-3973 allows a simple probate procedure called SUMMARY ADMINISTRATION for small estates. The statute does not give a dollar amount for the procedure, but requires that the value of the decedent's estate, must be not be greater than the sum of the following:

➤ reasonable funeral expenses

➤ homestead allowance ($18,000)

➤ family allowance ($12,000)

➤ exempt property   ($7,000)

➤ costs and expenses of administration

➤ reasonable and necessary medical and hospital expenses of the decedent's last illness ***

 **LAWYER**   ESTATES EXCEEDING $50,000

*** The cost of a person's last illness alone could be in the hundreds of thousands of dollars, but the Summary Administrative procedure was not designed to handle large estates. As a rule of thumb, if the entire value of the decedent's estate (less monies owed on any of the property) is greater than $50,000, then consult with an attorney experienced in Probate matter to determine whether the full Probate Administration is the better route to go.

APPOINTING THE PERSONAL REPRESENTATIVE IN A SUMMARY ADMINISTRATION

The first step in the Summary Administration procedure is to have someone appointed by the court as Personal Representative. If the decedent died testate, then the Personal Representative is named in the Will. If the Will was drafted in another state, then the Will may name an *Executor* to do the job. In either case, the person so named has the right to be appointed to settle the estate.

If the decedent died intestate, then the spouse has the right to be appointed as Personal RepresentativeIf the decedent was not married, then any of his heirs is entitled to be appointed as Personal Representative, provided that all the other heirs renounce or waive their right by filing an appropriate document with the Probate court (AZ 14-2303).

 **BENEFICIARY WHO IS NOT PERSONAL REPRESENTATIVE**

Arizona follows the Uniform Probate Code. The Code is designed to speed administration and reduce costs by giving the Personal Representative much autonomy. The downside is that with little court supervision the Personal Representative can do serious mischief.

If you are concerned about the ability of the Personal Representative to properly administer the estate, then do not sign a waiver, but consult with an attorney who is experienced in probate matters to discuss the feasibility of having the person of your choice to serve as Personal Representative.

If there is no disagreement about who is to be Personal Representative, then he/she needs to go to the Probate court in the county of the decedent's residence. If the decedent was not a resident of the state, then the Probate procedure can be in the county where the decedent owned real property (AZ 14-3201).

If you are going to be Personal Representative, then you may save time by first calling the Registrar and asking:
> *How do I get to the courthouse?*
> *When is the best time to meet with the registrar?*
> *What documents should I bring?*
> *How much money should I bring for the filing fee?*

Once the Registrar of the Probate court is satisfied that the estate qualifies for Summary Administration, he/she will issue Letters of Administration to the Personal Representative who then proceeds with the job of settling the decedent's estate.

FULL PROBATE ADMINISTRATION

If the decedent left real property or assets worth more than $50,000, then there needs to be a full Probate Administration. The procedure can take anywhere from 5 months to more than a year depending on the size of the Probate Estate. It is the Personal Representative's job to use the Probate Estate to pay all valid claims and then to distribute what is left to the proper beneficiary.

All of the decedent's debts are paid from the Probate Estate and not from Personal Representative's pocket; but if the Personal Representative makes a mistake then he may be responsible to pay for that mistake. For example, suppose the Personal Representative pays a debt that did not need to be paid — or if the Personal Representative transfers property to the beneficiaries too quickly and there were still taxes due on the estate. In such cases, the Personal Representative may be responsible to pay for such error.

The Personal Representative needs to employ an attorney to guide him through the process. It then becomes the job of the attorney for the Personal Representative to see to it that the estate is administered properly and without any personal liability to the Personal Representative. The cost of employing an attorney is a proper charge to the Probate Estate. The attorney usually works on an hourly basis, charging anywhere from $175/hour to $225/hour depending on the complexity of the case.

The Personal Representative is entitled to reasonable compensation for his efforts. The court usually allows between $10/hour to $20/hour, again depending on the complexity of the matter.

 **BENEFICIARY ALERT**

As explained on page 127, the Personal Representative operates much on his own. The beneficiary has the legal right to demand that the Personal Representative keep him informed as to how the probate is proceeding. If the estate is sizeable, then the beneficiary should consider employing his own attorney to check that things are done properly and in a timely manner. If you, as beneficiary, are not in a financial position to employ an attorney, then you can take the following steps to protect you interests:

FILE DEMAND FOR NOTICE
If a Personal Representative has not been appointed, then file a **DEMAND FOR NOTICE** with the clerk of the Superior Court in the county of the decedent's residence. This demand ensures that you will be notified once the case is opened.

REQUEST INVENTORY
The law requires that the Personal Representative file an inventory of all of the assets of the Probate estate within 90 days. But 90 days is a long time. The Personal Representative should be able to determine what assets are in the estate in half that time. You have the right to ask the court to have the Personal Representative to file an inventory in less than 90 days.

DEMAND SUFFICIENT BOND
Ask the Personal Representative, in writing, to give you copies of bank statements, brokerage account statements and all appraisals. Once you know the value of the estate, compare it to the value of the bond posted by the Personal Representative. If the bond is less than the value of the estate, then ask the court to have the bond increased.

DETERMINE FEES

Ask the Personal Representative whether he intends to charge a fee. Have him put the response in writing, even if his reply is that he will not charge a fee. If the Personal Representative says that he has not made up his mind, then ask him to do so within a given period of time.

Ask the Personal Representative to give you a copy of the retainer agreement that he signed with his attorney, so that you will know how much is being charged for legal fees. If the attorney is employed on an hourly basis, have the attorney give a written estimate of the time he expects to expend on the probate procedure.

HAVE THE ATTORNEY HANDLE THE FINANCES

Require that the Personal Representative's attorney have control of the estate check book. Ask that the decedent's mail be forwarded to the attorney's office. By doing so, the attorney will discover the decedent's assets. As an officer of the court, the attorney has a duty to report the existence of all assets to the court and to the beneficiaries.

Ask the attorney to confirm to you that he/she is receiving and reviewing the estate checking account and other depository assets of the estate.

DEMAND COPIES OF ALL TAX RETURNS

It is important that you receive copies of all tax returns that the Personal Representative is obliged to file. If the Personal Representative fails to file the decedent's final income tax return, or fails to pay estate taxes, or if he under reports a tax obligation, then you could later be called on to pay the decedent's taxes out of the proceeds that you receive. If you get a copy of the tax returns then you can check to see that the taxes were properly paid.

IT'S YOUR RIGHT - DON'T BE INTIMIDATED

You may feel uncomfortable being assertive with a friend or family member who is Personal Representative. Don't be. It's your money and your legal right to be kept informed. Be especially firm if the Personal Representative waives you off with:

"You've known me for years. Surely you trust me."

People who are trustworthy, don't ask to be trusted. They do what is right. The very fact that the Personal Representative is resisting is a red flag. In such cases you can explain that it is not a matter of trust, but a matter of what is your legal right.

If you are still getting an argument, then close the discussion with "I am prepared to bring this matter to the attention of the court" and then call a lawyer.

 THE OUT OF STATE RESIDENT

If the decedent had his principal residence in another state but owned property in Arizona, then the same problem arises; namely, where to conduct the probate procedure. If the decedent did not own property in the state of his residence, it may be possible to conduct the probate in Arizona, only. It is important to consult with an attorney in each state before making a decision.

 OUT OF STATE PROPERTY

If the decedent owned property in Arizona and in another state, you may need to have a probate procedure in Arizona and an *ancillary* (secondary) probate procedure in the other state. It could be done the other way around; namely, you could have the probate in the other state and the ancillary procedure in Arizona.

If probate is to be in another state, then the original Will will need to be delivered to the Probate court in that state. The Personal Representative (or next of kin, if no Will) should consult with an attorney in each state to determine the best course of action. Convenience and cost are important considerations, but you also need to consider that each state has its own tax structure and probate statutes. Ask each attorney whether the location of the probate procedure will have any effect on who is to inherit the property or how much the estate will be taxed.

HOW TO GET THE CONTENTS OF THE SAFE DEPOSIT BOX

If the decedent leased a safe deposit box together with another person, each with full authority to enter the box, then the co-lessee of the box can remove all of its contents. If, however, the decedent and another, both needed to be present in order to access the box, or if the decedent was the sole lessee of a safe deposit box, then some sort of probate procedure is necessary in order to get possession of the contents of the box.

If there is a full probate procedure or a Summary Administration then a Personal Representative will be appointed by the Probate court. The court will give the Personal Representative Letters of Administration saying that the Personal Representative has full authority to take possession of all of the assets that belonged to the decedent. If the decedent had a safe deposit box, then the Personal Representative can present the Letters of Administration to the bank or safe deposit box lessor, and they will give the Personal Representative access to the box and all of its contents.

If the decedent's property is being transferred by means of an Affidavit, then the Affidavit can be presented to the lessor of the safe deposit box. To prepare the Affidavit you will need to identify the contents of the box. See page 60 for information about how to obtain an inventory of the contents of the safe deposit box.

THE CHECK LIST

We have discussed many things that need to be done when someone dies in the state of Arizona. The next page contains a check list that you may find helpful.

You can check those items that you need to do, and then cross them off the list once they are done. We made the list as comprehensive as possible, so many items may not apply in your case. In such case, you can cross them off the list or mark them *N/A* (not applicable).

Things to do

FUNERAL ARRANGMENTS TO BE MADE
☐ AUTOPSY   ☐ ANATOMICAL GIFT
☐ DISPOSITION OF BODY OR ASHES

DEATH CERTIFICATE
☐ RECORD WITH COUNTY RECORDER
GIVE COPY TO: _____
_____

NOTICE OF DEATH
PEOPLE TO BE NOTIFIED _____

COMPANIES TO NOTIFY
☐ TELEPHONE COMPANY
   ☐ LOCAL CARRIER   ☐ LONG DISTANCE   ☐ CELLULAR
☐ NEWSPAPER (OBITUARY PRINTED)
☐ NEWSPAPER CANCELLED   ☐ deposit refund
☐ SOCIAL SECURITY
☐ INTERNET SERVER
☐ TELEVISION CABLE COMPANY
☐ ARIZONA POWER & LIGHT   ☐ deposit refund
☐ POST OFFICE
☐ OTHER UTILITIES (GAS, WATER)   ☐ deposit refund
☐ PENSION PLAN
☐ ANNUITY
☐ HEALTH INSURANCE COMPANY
☐ LIFE INSURANCE COMPANY
☐ HOME INSURANCE COMPANY
☐ MOTOR VEHICLE INSURANCE COMPANY
☐ CONDOMINIUM OR HOMEOWNER ASSOCIATION
☐ CREDIT CARD COMPANIES _____
   _____
   _____

Things to do

REMOVE DECEDENT AS BENEFICIARY OF:
- ☐ WILL
- ☐ INSURANCE POLICY
- ☐ PENSION PLAN
- ☐ BANK OR IRA ACCOUNT
- ☐ SECURITY

DEBTS

PAY DECEDENT'S DEBTS (AMOUNT & CREDITOR)

_____

COLLECT MONIES OWED TO DECEDENT (AMOUNT & DEBTOR)

_____

TAXES
- ☐ FILE FINAL FEDERAL INCOME TAX RETURN
- ☐ FILE FINAL STATE INCOME TAX RETURN
- ☐ RECEIVE INCOME TAX REFUND
- ☐ FILE ESTATE TAX RETURN

PROPERTY TO BE TRANSFERRED
- ☐ MOTOR VEHICLE
- ☐ PERSONAL EFFECTS
- ☐ MOTOR VEHICLE
- ☐ BANK ACCOUNT
- ☐ CREDIT UNION ACCOUNT
- ☐ IRA ACCOUNT
- ☐ SECURITIES
- ☐ BROKERAGE ACCOUNT
- ☐ INSURANCE PROCEEDS
- ☐ HOMESTEAD
- ☐ TIME SHARE
- ☐ OTHER REAL PROPERTY
- ☐ CONTENTS OF SAFE DEPOSIT BOX

OTHER THINGS TO DO

_____
_____
_____

CHAPTER 7
PRENEED ARRANGEMENTS

Death is a wake-up call because once someone close to us dies we are reminded of our own mortality. We realize that death can be put off, but the inevitable is inevitable. Although we cannot change the fact of our death, we have the power to control the circumstances of our death by making preneed arrangements.

You can make preneed arrangements so that you will be buried in the manner you wish and where you wish. You can also make arrangements that direct the kind of medical treatments you want to be given in the event you become seriously ill.

You can legally appoint someone to make your medical decisions in the event that you are too ill to speak for yourself. If you let that person know how you feel about life support systems, autopsies and anatomical gifts then that person will be authorized to act on your behalf and see to it that your wishes are carried out.

As this chapter will show, it is relatively simple and inexpensive to make such preneed arrangements.

MAKING BURIAL ARRANGEMENTS

When someone dies, it is common for the family to purchase one or more burial spaces near the decedent. You may wish to consider doing so at this time. If the decedent was buried in the family plot, then this is the time to take inventory of the number of spaces left and who in the family expects to use those spaces.

If all of the spaces are taken and if you plan to be cremated, then some cemeteries will allow an urn to be placed in an occupied family plot. You can call the cemetery and ask them to explain their policy as it relates to the burial of urns in currently occupied gravesites.

Most cemeteries have mausoleums where you can reserve a space for urns. Many cemeteries have a separate building called a *columbarium*, which is a building especially designed to store urns.

If you wish to have your ashes scattered then you need to let your next of kin know where and how this is to be done.

BURIAL OF VETERAN OR VETERAN'S SPOUSE

If you are an honorably discharged veteran, you have the right to be buried in a Veterans National Cemetery. You cannot reserve a gravesite in advance. If your Veteran spouse was buried in a Veterans National Cemetery then you have the right to be buried in that same gravesite unless soil conditions require a separate gravesite.

If you wish to be buried in a Veterans National Cemetery, then check on current availability (see page 16 for telephone numbers). Let your next of kin know your choice of cemetery.

To establish your eligibility your next of kin will need to provide the following information:

➢ the veteran's rank, serial, social security and VA claim numbers

➢ the branch of service; the date and place of entry into and separation from the service

The next of kin will also need to provide the VA with a copy of the veteran's official military discharge document bearing an official seal or a DD 214 form.

If you wish to be buried in a national cemetery, then make all of these items readily accessible to your family.

MAKING FUNERAL ARRANGEMENTS

PREARRANGED FUNERALS

If you are financially able, in addition to purchasing a burial space, consider purchasing a prearranged funeral plan. It will be easier on your family emotionally and financially if you make your own funeral arrangements. If you do not have sufficient cash on hand for the kind of funeral you desire, then many funeral directors offer an installment payment plan.

Once you decide on a plan, the funeral director will present you with a Prearranged Funeral Agreement. The Agreement is a legally binding contract so it is important that you take the time to read it before signing. If the contract is written in "legalese" then either consult with your attorney before signing it or ask as many questions of the funeral director as is necessary to make the terms of the agreement clear to you. If you are not satisfied with the way a certain section of the contract is written then add an addendum to the agreement that explains, in plain English, your understanding of that passage.

If you are concerned about something that is not mentioned in the contract, then insist that the contract be amended to include that item, for example:

What if the funeral home goes out of business?

Arizona laws are designed to protect the purchaser of a prearranged funeral plan. Arizon statute 32-1391.02 (C) requires that funeral establishments protect funds paid by the consumer of a prearranged funeral plan either by insurance or by placement of the prepaid funds into a trust account.

FUNDS PROTECTED BY TRUST

If the funds are placed in a trust account, then each prearranged funeral agreement must contain a "NOTICE TO PURCHASER" that states where the trust account is located and the amount of money the establishment will charge for servicing the account (AZ 32-1391.09).

Does the contract cover all costs?

If the funds are placed in a trust account then the prearranged funeral agreement must itemize the funeral goods and services to be provided AND to identify any funeral, burial, cemetery or crematory expense that is not covered under the Agreement (AZ 32-1391.09 (B)).

If you have not purchased a burial space, then that cost needs to be factored in.

Of course these safeguards may fail if you are not doing business with a reputable funeral home. It is prudent to take the time to call the investigation division of the Arizona State Board of Funeral Directors. **602-542-3095.** Ask if the funeral establishment is licensed and whether any complaints have been filed against them.

Suppose you die in another state or country?

It is a good idea to have the contract spell out what provision will be made in the event that you move to another state or in the event you happen to die in another state or country. Many funeral homes are part of a national funeral service corporation with funeral homes located throughout the United States, so this is not usually a problem.

What will it cost if you cancel the agreement?
Arizona statute 32-1391.07 gives the purchaser of a prearranged funeral agreement the right to cancel the agreement for a full refund within 3 days after signing the agreement.   The funeral establishment must return the monies within 5 business days after receiving the request. The agreement can be cancelled by the purchaser after the initial 3 day period, but the funeral establishment may retain a service fee.   You need to find out what it will cost if you decide to cancel at a later date.

Can the plan be changed?
It could happen that, for one reason or another, the funeral establishment is not able to deliver the goods or services, for example:
➢   a missing body or one that cannot be recovered
➢   burial by another facility because your heirs were
      unaware of the arrangement you made
➢   burial in another country
If the funeral establishment does not provide the goods and services within 30 days of death, then all remaining trust funds must be immediately paid to the decedent's estate (AZ 32-1391.08).

But what if you or your heirs want to change the plan in some way? Arizona law 32-1391.07 (A) gives anyone you designate on the prearranged funeral agreement, the right to terminate the agreement after you die and to receive a refund.   But perhaps your heirs just want to modify the plan, perhaps purchase a more expensive plan and pay the difference or change to a lesser plan and receive a refund.

Sometimes a person buys a very modest plan and the children decide to add their own funds to have their parent buried in the "proper" style.

Consider that in today's market, it is not uncommon for a prearranged funeral plan to cost several thousand dollars. A top end funeral complete with solid bronze casket can cost upwards of $40,000. In such case, there might be a temptation for the heirs to down grade the plan.

Such was the case with Lester. His mother was always a difficult woman with a personality that can only be described as "sour." Her husband deserted her after four years of marriage leaving her to raise their son, Lester, by herself. Once Lester was grown, his mother made it clear that she had done her job and now he was on his own.

Lester could have used some help. He married and had three children. One of his children suffered with asthma and it was a constant struggle to keep up with the medical bills.

Lester's mother believed in being good to herself. She did not intend to, nor did she, leave much money when she died. She wanted to die as she had lived, namely "in style." Just before she died she purchased a funeral plan and paid close to $9,000 for it. She felt comfortable when the funeral director explained how her funds were being placed into a trust fund for safekeeping until her death. She wasn't aware of the Arizona law that gave heirs the right to terminate that funeral plan.
Lester knew about the law.
You know the ending to this story.

Mona might have done better to purchase burial insurance payable to a funeral home for the specific purpose of burying her in the manner she wished.

PURCHASING BURIAL INSURANCE

If you are concerned that you get the exact type of funeral that you want, with no changes, then you might consider purchasing a life insurance policy payable to your estate with instructions in your Will that the money from this policy is to be used to purchase the type of funeral you wish as directed in your Will. This ensures that no one can revoke your instructions, because the distribution of the insurance funds to the funeral home is court supervised.

Many insurance companies have specific burial insurance policies, so you might investigate such insurance plans. The cost of the policy might be less than purchasing a Preneed plan. You could insure yourself with sufficient monies to cover the cost of the burial and other miscellaneous expenses such as paying for a lunch after the burial, or paying the airfare for a family member to attend the service.

If you wish to purchase burial insurance, but you do not want to trigger a probate procedure for a single insurance policy, then you could name a trusted family member as the beneficiary of the policy. It is important that the person who is to receive the insurance funds clearly understands why he/she is named as beneficiary of the policy. It is equally important that the beneficiary agree to use the monies for the intended purpose. It isn't so much that a family member is not trustworthy as it is that they may not understand what you intended — especially in those cases where other funds are available to pay for the funeral. Too often insurance funds are left to a sibling who then refuses to contribute to the cost of the funeral saying in effect "Dad wanted me to have this money — that's why he left it to me."

To avoid a misunderstanding, put it in writing. It need not be a formal contract. It could be something as simple as a letter to the insurance beneficiary, with copies to your next of kin, saying something like:

Dear Romita and William,
I purchased a $10,000 insurance policy today naming you both as beneficiaries. As we discussed, this money is to be used to pay for the following:
  - *my funeral and gravesite*
  - *my headstone*
  - *perpetual care for my grave*
  - *airfare for each of my grandchildren to attend the funeral*
  - *dinner for the family after the wake*
  - *lunch for the family after the funeral*
If there is any money left over, please divide it between you as my thanks for all the effort spent on my behalf.
Love, Dad

P.S. I'm sending a copy of this letter to your sister, Adrianne so she will understand the purpose of the insurance policy.

Whether or not you arrange to pay for your burial or funeral, you need to let your next of kin know your feelings about the burial procedure. Let your family know whether you wish to be cremated or buried. If you wish to have a religious service, then let your family know the type of service and where it is to be held. Let the family know where you wish to be buried, or if you intend to be cremated, then where to place the ashes.

AUTOPSIES

As discussed in Chapter 1, some autopsies are optional. If you have strong feelings about allowing an optional autopsy or not allowing the procedure, then let your family know how you feel.

ANATOMICAL GIFTS

If you wish to make an anatomical gift, you can make the donation by signing a document of gift. That document of gift can be attached or imprinted onto your Arizona driver's license.

If you are aged, and in poor health, the local Organ Procurement Organization will probably not consider your body for transplantation of body parts, but you can still donate your body for education and research. If you wish to make such as donation, then you can write or call the University of Arizona. See page 7 for their address and telephone number. They will send you an information package and the forms necessary to make the donation.

If you are opposed to making an anatomical gift, then let your family know how you feel. Of course, there are problems with just telling someone how you feel about your burial arrangements, autopsies, and anatomical gifts:

YOU TELL THE WRONG PERSON

The person you confide in may not be present when the arrangements are made. For example, if you tell your spouse what arrangements to make then he/she may die before you do — or you could die simultaneously in a car or plane crash.

THE PERSON DOES NOT CARRY OUT YOUR WISHES

The person you tell may not understand what you said or perhaps they hear only what they want to hear. An example that comes to mind is the mother who constantly complained that she felt like a burden to her children. She would often say "When I die, just burn my body and throw my ashes out to sea." Her children paid no attention. When she died she was given a full funeral and placed in the family plot. They never asked, nor did they even consider, whether their mother really did want be cremated.

WHO WANTS TO TALK ABOUT IT?

For many people the main problem with telling someone what to do when you die is talking about your death. It may be an uncomfortable, if not unpleasant, subject for you to bring up, and for your family to discuss. If this is the case, then consider putting the information in writing and give the instructions to the person who will have the job of carrying out your wishes.

PREPARING A HEALTH CARE DIRECTIVE

To make your written instructions legally enforceable consider signing a *Health Care Directive*. A Health Care Directive is a document that gives instructions about the medical treatment you wish to be given in the event that you are too ill to give consent for your medical treatment. Two kinds of Health Care Directives are the Living Will and the Health Care Power of Attorney:

A *Living Will* is Health Care Directive that states whether you do (or do not) wish life support systems to be used in the event that you are dying and there is no hope for your recovery. A *Health Care Surrogate* is someone you appoint to carry out these instructions and make your medical decisions in the event that you are too ill to speak for yourself. You can appoint a Health Care Surrogate by signing a document called a *Health Care Power of Attorney.*

Arizona statute 36-3262 contains a sample form for a Living Will. Arizona Statute 36-3224 has a sample Health Care Power of Attorney. This form has sections that you can use to express your wishes regarding autopsies and anatomical gifts. You can look up these statutes at a public or courthouse library or you can down load them from the internet:

ARIZONA STATUTE WEB SITE
http://www.azleg.state.az.us

Numerous religious and civic organizations offer literature relating to the organization's position on the topic of Health Care Directives. Many religious and civic organizations offer Health Care Directives to their members, either free of charge, or at a nominal fee.

If you do not appoint someone to act as your surrogate and you are too sick to make your own medical decisions, then the person authorized to make medical decisions for you is established by Arizona statute 36-3231, in the following order of priority:

1. The spouse (unless legally separated)
2. An adult child. If more than one child, then the health care provider must seek the consent of the majority of those who are reasonably available for consultation.
3. A parent
4. The patient's domestic partner, provided no other person has assumed any financial responsibility for the patient
5. A brother or sister
6. A close friend

If this order of priority is not as you wish, then it is important to sign a Health Care Power of Attorney and appoint the person of your choice to act as your Surrogate. You can also use the Health Care Power of Attorney to completely bar someone from making your medical decisions.

Consider the example of George. His wife suffered from Alzheimer's disease. He cared for her at home for as long as he was able, but finally, it was too much for him and he placed her in a local nursing facility. He and his two daughters visited her frequently, even though she scarcely recognized them.

George met Emily on one of his visits to the nursing home. Her husband suffered from multiple strokes and was at the same nursing home. George and Emily had much in common. After visiting with their respective spouses they would go to the local coffee shop and visit with each other. One thing led to another, and soon they were an item.

George's daughters were not happy with the coupling. They criticized everything about Emily, from the way she dressed to her table manners . When Emily moved in with George, his daughters made cutting remarks about Emily's moral character. Emily didn't take it personally. She believed the girls were more concerned about their inheritance than George's happiness. A second marriage might cut into what they already considered to be rightfully theirs.

Not that George and Emily planned to wed. They both loved their respective spouses and had no intention of trying to obtain a divorce. Their understanding was that if and when they both were single, they would discuss marriage at that time.

George and Emily were most compatible. Their affection for each other increased over the five years that they lived together. Each was happier than they had ever been before, until the day of the accident. George had a stroke while driving a car. He was seriously injured and lapsed into a coma. The prognosis was not encouraging. The doctors said George would die unless they put him on a ventilator and inserted a feeding tube. Even with these life support systems, they were not promising that he would survive.

Emily pleaded to keep him alive.   "Let's try everything. If he doesn't improve we can always discontinue the life support systems later."   George's daughters did not see it that way.   "Why torture him with needles and tubes? Let him pass on peacefully."

George never signed a Living Will, so no one knew how he felt about life support systems. He never appointed any one to be his Surrogate in the event he was unable to make his own medical decisions. In the absence of a Health Care Power of Attorney the doctors had no choice but to follow Arizona law.   The daughters were 2nd in priority. Emily was 4th.

George died.

CHAPTER 8
EVERYMAN'S ESTATE PLAN

The first six chapters of this book describe how to wind up the affairs of the decedent. As you read these chapters, you learned about the kinds of problems that can occur when someone dies. It is relatively simple for you to make an estate plan so that your family members are not burdened with similar problems. An *estate plan* is the arranging of one's finances to reduce (if not eliminate) probate costs and estate taxes, so that your beneficiaries inherit property quickly and at little cost.

If you think that only wealthy people need to prepare an estate plan, think again. Each year, heirs of relatively modest estates, spend thousands of dollars to settle an estate. A bit of planning could have eliminated most, if not all, of the hassle and cost suffered by those families.

The suggestions in this chapter are designed to assist the average person in preparing a practical and inexpensive estate plan, so we have named this chapter **EVERYMAN'S ESTATE PLAN**. Once you create your own estate plan, you can rest assured that your family will not be left with more problems than happy memories of you.

HOW TO AVOID PROBATE

In Arizona probate procedures for small estates are relatively simple but they can be time consuming and stressful. If you have a small estate and only one or two beneficiaries, then it is not all that difficult to arrange your finances so that there will be no need for any kind of probate procedure when you die.

BANK ACCOUNTS

You can arrange to have all of your bank accounts, (savings, checking, certificates of deposit and share accounts) titled so that the money goes directly to your heirs when you die. For example, suppose all you have is a bank account with a balance of $40,000 and you want to have this go to your son and daughter when you die. You might think that a simple solution is to put each child's name on the account. But making it a joint account may not be the best solution:

THE JOINT ACCOUNT
The Joint or Multiple Party bank account gives each joint owner of the account complete access to the funds in that account (AZ 14-6201(5)).

POTENTIAL LIABILITY
If you hold property jointly with one of your adult children and that child is sued or gets a divorce, then the child may need to disclose their ownership of the joint account. In such a case, you may find yourself spending money to prove that the account was established for convenience only, and that all of the money in that account really belongs to you.

SECURITY/OVERREACHING

If you set up a joint account with your child, then the child can withdraw funds that you did not authorize to be withdrawn. If you open a joint account with two of your children, then after your death the first child to the bank may decide to withdraw all of the money. Both of these acts are illegal, but in such situations families are reluctant to do anything more than become very angry with the offender.

MINOR CHILD

Arizona statute 6-235 allows a bank deposit to be held jointly with, and payable to, a minor, but would you want that minor child to be able to go to the bank upon your death and remove all the money?

THE POD/IN TRUST FOR ACCOUNT

There is a simple solution to the problem of securing your account, yet ensuring your heirs get the money without going through probate, and that is to open a "PAY-ON-DEATH" account, or an account that is held "IN TRUST FOR" or "FOR THE BENEFIT OF" a beneficiary. During your lifetime your beneficiary has no right to the funds in the account. You are free to change the beneficiary of the account without asking the beneficiary's permission to do so (AZ 14-6211 (B)).

Once you die, the beneficiary can immediately access the funds, however, as explained on page 69, if you die with much debt, your Personal Representative has the right to require that the funds in any bank account that you might own, be used to pay those debts.

THE UNIFORM TRANSFERS TO MINORS ACT

If the intended beneficiary of your bank account is a minor, you can instruct the financial institution that you want the funds to be held in conformity with the ARIZONA UNIFORM TRANSFERS TO MINORS ACT. If you die before the beneficiary is 18, the financial institution will keep the monies invested until the beneficiary turns 18. At that time the monies will be given to the beneficiary (AZ 14-7670).

SECURITIES

You can purchase securities, or set up a securities brokerage account, in the same manner as a bank account, namely you can hold the securities jointly with rights of survivorship or you can hold the property in your name only and arrange to have the security transferred to one or more beneficiaries when you die. Either way the property will be transferred without the need for a probate procedure.

To have a security transferred upon your death, you can instruct the transfer agent to "transfer on death" ("TOD") to your intended beneficiary. You can also use the "POD" designation. The laws regarding the TOD account are similar to those for the POD account:

⇨   The beneficiary does not own the security until the owner of the security dies. During his lifetime the owner is free to change beneficiaries without asking the beneficiary's permission to do so.

⇨   Once the owner of the security dies the security is transferred to the named beneficiary.

(Arizona statutes 14-6305, 6306, 6307)

If the beneficiary is a minor, you can name an adult or a trust company to be custodian of the security, should you die before the child is an adult, by registering the security in the adult's (or company's) name "as custodian for _____ (name of minor) under the Arizona Uniform Transfers to Minors Act (AZ 14-7659).

 **BUSINESS INTERESTS**

If you own a business, be it a sole proprietorship, partnership or close corporation, you need to make provision for the orderly transfer of your business interest in the event you die suddenly. An attorney who is experienced in business law (corporation, banking, bankruptcy, commercial law, franchise law, etc.) can offer suggestions as to the best method of ensuring that the business continues its operation, or terminates in an orderly fashion — whichever is applicable in your case.

If you cannot afford to employ an attorney at this time, then consult with your accountant. Let your accountant know who is to have access to your business records in the event of your incapacity or death. Discuss how company debts will be paid and how best to distribute the company assets to your heirs, in case of your death. If it is your intent that the business continue in your absence, you might consider purchasing key man insurance on your life to compensate the company for any loss suffered because of your absence. See page 40 for an explanation of key man insurance.

MOTOR VEHICLES

As discussed in chapter 5, if you own a motor vehicle with someone and the title is in the name of that person "AND" you, then if one of you dies, the other may need to go through a probate procedure to determine who now owns the decedent's share of the motor vehicle. If you wish the motor vehicle to go to the surviving owner, then have the title read "OR" or "AND/OR."

If you are thinking about holding title to a car jointly with someone just to avoid probate, then consider the problem of liability. If either owner is in an accident with the car, then both are liable for any damage that is done. If you are single, the better route is to hold title to the car in your name only and make a gift of the car in your Will.

REAL PROPERTY

As explained in Chapter 5, if you own real property together with another, then who will own the property upon your death depends on how the Grantee is identified on the face of the deed. If you compare the Grantee clause of the deed to the examples on pages 89 through 93 you can determine who will inherit your property should you die. If you are not satisfied with the way the property will be inherited, then you need to consult with an attorney to change the deed so that it will conform to your wishes.

If you own the property in your name only, and you have more than $50,000 in equity in the property, then once you die, there will need to be a formal probate procedure before the property can be transferred to the proper beneficiary. If your main objective is to avoid probate, then you can have an attorney change the deed so that once you die the property descends to your beneficiary without the need for probate. Of course, there are trade-offs:

JOINT OWNERSHIP WITH RIGHTS OF SURVIVORSHIP

You can have your deed changed so that you and a beneficiary are joint owners with rights of survivorship. If you do so, you will avoid probate of the property, but you will not be able to sell that property during your lifetime without the beneficiary's permission. And if the beneficiary gives permission and the property is sold, the beneficiary may demand "his half" of the proceeds of the sale.

Still another problem is the ability of your joint owner to handle finances. If the joint owner is unable to manage his/her affairs because of accident or ill health, and you want to sell the property, then you will need to ask a court to declare the person to be incapacitated and to appoint a conservator to sign the deed on behalf of the joint owner. Conservatorship proceeding are both time consuming and expensive. Once a conservatorship is established it continues until the person is restored to health or dies. If you do not hold the property jointly with another then you need not worry about their ability to conduct business.

LIFE ESTATE INTEREST

You can transfer the property to a beneficiary and keep a Life Estate interest for yourself. This means that you have the right to occupy the property for so long as you live. Once you die your beneficiary will own the property without any need for probate, but again there is a downside:

▷ You cannot sell the property during your lifetime without the beneficiary agreeing to the sale.

▷ If you sell the property, the beneficiary is entitled to some portion of the proceeds of the sale.

▷ If you or your beneficiary become incapacitated, then the property cannot be sold unless a conservator is appointed.

GIFT OF HOMESTEAD TO BENEFICIARY

Some people think it a good idea to simply transfer their homestead to their children to avoid probate, but this just creates a new set of problems. If you put the deed in the beneficiary's name and that property is your homestead, you will lose creditor protection associated with your homestead. Arizona statute 33-1101 offers homestead protections against being taken by a creditor. If you are sued and lose, and if the value of your homestead is less than $100,000, the creditor cannot force you to sell the property to pay the debt (unless, of course, the money you owe is for a mortgage or improvements to your home). Arizona statute 33-1123 also exempts your household furnishings and appliances up to $4,000 in value from the claims of your creditors.

If you transfer property to a beneficiary and he/she does not occupy that property as their homestead, then there is no creditor protection for your beneficiary as well. Your homestead could be lost if the beneficiary runs into serious financial difficulties or if the beneficiary gets a divorce and the property somehow becomes part of the settlement.

 **TAX/MEDICAID CONSEQUENCES OF GIFT OF REAL PROPERTY**

Before you make a real estate tranfer, be it joint interest, life estate or outright gift, you need to consider the tax and Medicaid issues:

⊠ POSSIBLE CAPITAL GAINS TAX
If you gift the property to a beneficiary and continue to live there until you die, then when the beneficiary sells the property there might be a capital gains tax. The beneficiary will be taxed on the increase in value from the time of your purchase until it is sold. If you do not make the transfer during your lifetime and the beneficiary inherits the property, there is no capital gains tax. The beneficiary inherits the property at the market value as of your date of death. The beneficiary can sell the property at that time without any tax consequence.

⊠ POSSIBLE GIFT TAX
If the value of the transfer is worth more than $10,000 you need to file a gift tax return. For most of us, this is not a problem because no gift tax needs to be paid unless the value of the property (plus the value of all gifts in excess of $10,000 that you gave over your lifetime) exceed the Estate Tax Unified Credit. (Currently $675,000. See page 34 for the table of values.)

⊠ POSSIBLE LOSS OF MEDICAID BENEFITS
If you transfer property, then depending upon the value of the transfer, you could be disqualified from receiving Medicaid benefits for up to 3 years from the date of transfer. The federal and state rules that determine the period of ineligibility are complex. If nursing care may be an issue in the future, then it is best to consult with an Elder Law attorney to prepare a Medicaid Estate Plan.

| Special Situation | OUT OF STATE PROPERTY |

Each state is in charge of the way property located in that state is transferred. If you own property in another state (or country) then you need to consult with an attorney in that state (or country) to determine how that property will be transferred to your beneficiaries once you die. Most state laws are similar to Arizona, namely, property held as JOINT TENANTS WITH RIGHTS OF SURVIVORSHIP or a LIFE ESTATE INTEREST goes to your beneficiary without the need for probate. If you own property with your spouse in a non-community property state, should either of you die, the other owns the property 100% without a need for probate.

If you own property in another state in your name only, or as a TENANT IN COMMON then a probate procedure will most likely need to be held in that state. If it is necessary for your heirs to have probate procedure in Arizona, then they will need a second procedure in the state in which the property is located. The second probate procedure is called *ancillary administration.* This may have the effect of doubling the cost of probate to your heirs.

Still another problem is the matter of taxes. Arizona's Estate taxes are tied to the Federal Estate tax. If your estate is too small to pay Federal Estate taxes (see page 34 for the schedule), then you pay no Arizona Estate tax. This may not be the case with other states; so in addition to paying extra for the second probate procedure, your heirs may need to pay Estate taxes in the state in which the property is located. If such is the case, you may wish to consult with an attorney for suggestions about how to set up your estate plan to avoid these problems.

A TRUST MAY BE THE SOLUTION (OR NOT)

As we have seen, many of the ways to avoid probate involve methods with undesirable trade-offs. One way to avoid some of these potential problems is to set up a trust. If you have substantial assets, then you probably have heard this suggestion from your financial planner or attorney, or accountant. Even people of fairly modest means are being encouraged by these professionals to use a trust as the basis of their estate plan. But even trusts have their downside. But before getting into that, let's first discuss what a trust is and how it works:

SETTING UP A TRUST

To create a trust, an attorney prepares the trust document in accordance with the client's needs and desires. The person who signs the document is referred to as the **Grantor** or **Settlor** of the Trust. The trust document identifies who is to be the Trustee (caretaker) of property placed in the trust. Usually the Grantor appoints himself as Trustee so that he is in total control of property that he places into the trust. The trust document names a Successor Trustee who will take over the management of the trust property should the Trustee become disabled or die.

Once the trust document is properly signed, the Grantor transfers property into the trust. The Grantor does this by changing the name on the account from that of the Grantor to that of the Trustee. For example, if ELAINE RICHARDS sets up a trust naming herself as trustee, and she wishes to place her bank account into the trust then all she need do is instruct the bank to change the name on the account from ELAINE RICHARDS to ELAINE RICHARDS, TRUSTEE. Once the change is made, all the money in the bank account becomes trust property. Elaine (wearing her trustee hat) still has total control of the account, taking money out and putting money in as she sees fit.

The trust document states how the trust property is to be managed during Elaine's lifetime. If the trust is a Revocable Living Trust, then it will say that Elaine has the power to terminate the trust at any time and have all trust property returned to her. Should Elaine become disabled or die, then her Successor Trustee will take possession of the trust funds and manage (or distribute them) according to the directions Elaine gave in the trust document. If the trust says that once Elaine dies, the property is to be given to a beneficiary, then the Successor Trustee will do so; and in most cases without a probate procedure. If the trust directs the Successor Trustee to hold property in trust to care for a member of Elaine's family, then the Successor Trustee will do so.

THE GOOD PART

Setting up a trust has many good features:

☆ CARE OF YOUR PROPERTY: If you become disabled or too aged to handle your finances, then you do not need to worry about who will care for your property because you have named someone you trust to be your Successor Trustee.

☆ CARE OF FAMILY MEMBER: If you make provision in your trust to care for a child or a family member after you die, then your Successor Trustee can do so. If the family member is immature or a born spender, you can set up a Spendthrift Trust to protect him from squandering his inheritance. The Successor Trustee can see to it that the trust funds are used to pay for the family member's education or living expenses, and nothing else.

☆ AVOID PROBATE: You may be able to avoid probate by having your Successor Trustee distribute the trust property to your beneficiaries when you die. If you have property in other states, then your Successor Trustee may be able to distribute the property without going through a probate procedure in that state.

☆ TAX SAVINGS

There can be substantial Estate tax savings if you are married and you and your spouse each set up your own trust. For example, suppose you and your spouse together have an estate worth one million dollars. You can each set up your own trust with $500,000. Each trust can provide that if one of you dies, the surviving spouse can use the income from the deceased partner's trust for living expenses. Once the surviving spouse dies, all of the monies in the two trusts can be distributed, with no estate taxes due on either trust. By doing this, you each take advantage of your own Unified Tax Credit.

If you don't separate your monies, then if one of you dies the surviving spouse has all of the money with only one deduction. For the year 2001, the credit is $675,000. If the Estate tax rate at that time is 31%, then the beneficiaries will pay over $100,000 in Estate taxes.

For married people of means, it makes good sense to establish a trust. Others need to consider the downside:

⊠ TAXES MAY STILL BE A PROBLEM

While the Grantor is operating the trust as Trustee, all of the property held in a Revocable Living Trust is taxed as if the Grantor were holding that property in his/her own name. If the value of the trust property exceeds the Grantor's Unified Tax Credit, then unless the Grantor takes some other Estate Planning strategy, taxes will be due and owing from the trust assets once the Grantor dies.

⊠ NO CREDITOR PROTECTION

Because property held in a Revocable Living Trust is freely accessible to the Grantor, it is likewise accessible to his creditors both before and after death. If the Grantor dies owing money then the trust funds can be used to pay for those debts (AZ 14-7705 A)

⊠ COST AND COMPLEXITY

A trust is a fairly complex document, often 20 pages (or more) long and written in "legalese." It may take considerable time and effort on your part to understand it. Because of the complexity of the document and the fact that it is custom designed for you, a trust may cost several hundred dollars. If a trust is being drafted for a married couple, then the cost can well exceed a thousand dollars.

It may also be expensive to maintain the trust should you become disabled or die. Your Successor Trustee has the right to charge for his duties as trustee, as well as to charge for any specialized services performed, such as fees to manage the trust portfolio, and accounting fees.

⊠ PROBATE MIGHT STILL BE NECESSARY

The trust only works for those items that you place in the trust. If you have property that is held jointly with another, then when you die, that property will go to the joint owner and not to the trust. If you purchase some real property in your own name and neglect to put it in your trust, there will need to be a probate procedure to determine the beneficiary of that property.

MAYBE PROBATE ISN'T ALL THAT BAD

If you hold all of your property jointly or in trust, you may be able to avoid probate and have your property go directly to your heirs. But you may have reason not to choose either of these methods. Setting up a trust may be too expensive for you at this time. You may not want to hold property jointly because of security reasons, or perhaps just to retain your independence. You may not want your property to go to someone automatically. You may want the flexibility of having your property distributed according to the directions in your Will; and then having the flexibility of changing your Will whenever you wish.

If you want money to go to several charities or to a minor child, then it may be better to make a Will rather than hold money"jointly" or in a POD or TOD account with just verbal instructions to your beneficiary about how you want the funds distributed when you die.

For example, if you hold all of your money and property jointly with your child, then the child is the legal owner of your property as of your date of death. If you tell your child to use some of that money for your grandchild's education, then that puts an unreasonable burden on your child because you were not specific as to exactly how much of that joint account was to be used for the child's education. Also you did not say how to use the money. Is the money for tuition only? Can the money be used to pay the child's living expenses?

Even if you give your child specific instructions about how the money is to be spent, and even if your child is honorable, and with the best intentions, it may be that your grandchild gets none of the money, because your child is sued or falls upon hard times and is forced to use that money to pay outstanding debts.

If you keep your property in your own name and leave a Will giving a certain amount of money for the grandchild, then your grandchild will know exactly how much money you left and the purpose of that gift. If your grandchild is a minor at the time you make your Will you can appoint a person or a financial institution to serve as custodian of the gift under the Arizona Uniform Transfers to Minors Act. The person or institution you name as custodian has the right to refuse to serve as custodian so it is important to discuss the appointment before naming anyone in your Will to serve in that capacity.

PREPARING A WILL

Some people think they do not need to prepare a Will until they are very old and about to die. But according to reports published by the National Center for Health Statistics (a division of the U.S. Department of Health and Human Services) 2 of every 10 people who die in any given year are under the age of 60. Many will think that 20% is a small number until it hits close to home as it did with a couple who were having difficulty conceiving a child. They went from doctor to doctor until they met someone who was just beginning his practice. With his knowledge of the latest advances in medicine, he was able to help them. The birth of their child was a moment of joy and gratitude. They asked a nurse to take a picture of them all together — the happy couple, the newborn child and the doctor who made it all happen. Happiness radiated from the picture, but one of them would be dead within six months.

You might think it was the child. An infant's life is so fragile. SIDS and all manner of childhood diseases can threaten a little one. But no, he grew up to be a healthy young man.

If you looked at the picture, you might guess the husband. Overweight, stressed out. His ruddy complexion suggested high blood pressure. He looked like he had a heart-attack-prone type A personality. But he was fine and went on to enjoy raising his son.

Probably the wife. She had such a difficult time with the pregnancy and the delivery was especially hard. Perhaps it was all too much for her. No, she recovered and later had two more children.

It was the doctor who was killed in a three car collision.

Though we all agree, that one never knows, still many think that no Will is necessary because they have arranged their finances so that all of their property goes to their intended beneficiary automatically and without the need for probate. Others don't bother with a Will because they know about the Laws of Intestate Succession and that's the way they want their property distributed anyway.

Even if you are satisfied with the way your estate will be distributed, you may want to have Will, so that you get to choose who will be in charge of handling your affairs once you die (your Personal Representative). If you don't have a Will and a probate procedure is necessary, the court will choose someone for the job (see Page 25).

Still another benefit to making a Will is that you can make provision for who will get your personal property, including your car. Without a Will, your Personal Representative gets to make these decisions. With a Will you can make provision for the care of your child or grandchild. You can even provide for the care of your pet as these next few pages will show.

If you decide to prepare a Will you can write one out by yourself but if you want to be certain that your Will is enforceable in this state or any where else, then it is advisable to seek the counsel of an attorney. If not, you might include something in your Will that could be read two different ways, or you might include something that is against Arizona law, such as trying to keep your spouse from inheriting anything at all.

CHOOSING A PERSONAL REPRESENTATIVE

The position of Personal Representative is a position of trust. Your Personal Representative is the person who takes charge of all of your affairs once you die. It is the Personal Representative's job to distribute your personal effects. If there is any dispute about items of sentimental value, then its his/her job to distribute the items equitably. It is the Personal Representative's job to take possession of all of your probate assets and use as much of them as is necessary to pay all your final bills. Once your bills are paid, then the Personal Representative has the duty to distribute whatever is left to your residuary beneficiaries.

If you make a Will, then you get to choose who will handle these important functions. You also get to choose an alternate Personal Representative in the event that the person you chose is unable or unwilling to do the job. You also get to decide whether you want a Probate court to supervise your Personal Representative:

The state of Arizona has two types of probate procedures: *Supervised Administration* and *Unsupervised Administration*. In a Supervised Administration, the Personal Representative is responsible to the court as well as to all interested parties (AZ 14-3501). A judge will supervise the distribution of your estate. Any deviation from the instructions in your Will can be made only for good cause and with court approval. If you wish to have a court oversee the distribution of your estate, then have your Will state that you wish a Supervised Administration. If your Will does not specifically state that the probate is to be Supervised, then it will be Unsupervised.

The Personal Representative of an Unsupervised Administration has the same duties and responsibilities as he would in a Supervised Administration. The only difference is that in an Unsupervised Administration the court is not "looking over his shoulder" to be sure that your wishes are carried out (AZ 14-3501).

If your Will does not request a Supervised Administration and for some reason the beneficiaries feel that they need the protection of the court, then they can petition (ask) the court for a Supervised Administration.   And vice versa. If your Will directs a Supervised Administration and the beneficiaries of your Will decide court supervision is unnecessary, then they can request an Unsupervised Administration . In both cases, the judge will weigh all of the facts and then decide what is best for all concerned (AZ 14-3502).

MAKE A GIFT OF YOUR CAR

It is easier to transfer the car after your death, if you name someone in your Will to inherit the car. If you do not name someone, then your heirs may need to agree about who will take the car, and how the rest of the heirs can be equitably compensated. This could lead to unnecessary arguments.

If your estate is probated and a Personal Representative is appointed, and you do not make a specific gift of your car in your Will, then the Personal Representative decides what to do with the car. He/she can decide to sell the car and include the proceeds of the sale in the estate funds to be distributed to your residuary beneficiaries — or he/she can give the car to a beneficiary as part of that beneficiary's share of the estate.

FOR PET LOVERS

A woman died at peace,
leaving her fortune
and care of her cat to her niece.
Alas, the fortune and the cat
Soon disappeared after that.

You could make a simple provision in your Will for the care of your pet, but the moral of the above limerick, is that just leaving your money to someone to do the job may not be the best route to go.

 ## TRUST FOR CARE OF PET

Arizona statute 14-2907 states that a trust established for the care of a pet is valid. If you are serious about caring for your pet after your death, you can employ an attorney to set up a separate trust for the care of your pet or you can include a trust for your pet in your Will.

You can appoint someone to be trustee of the funds and another to serve as the custodian of your pet. The trust document will direct the trustee to pay sufficient monies to the custodian for the care of the pet. You also need to name a beneficiary (a person or charitable organization) to receive whatever may remain in the trust after the pet dies. You can ask the trustee and the beneficiary to regularly check on the pet to see to it that the pet is treated humanely, if not benevolently.

CARE OF PETS (Continued)

If you don't have the resources to set up a trust to care for your pet, you can still ask a fellow pet lover to care for the animal. If no one among your circle of family and friends is able to do so, then ask your pet's veterinarian to consider starting an "Orphaned Pet Service" to assist in finding new homes for pets who lose their owners. Veterinarians often meet people who would welcome a new pet into their lives. It is good public relations and a potential source of income. People can make provision in their Will to pay the Veterinarian to care for the pet until a suitable family can be found.

That is a more humane approach than the, all to common practice, of putting a pet "to sleep" rather than have the pet suffer the loss of his master. And in at least one case, that reasoning backfired:

Eleanor always had a pet in the house. After her husband died, her two poodles were her constant companions. When Eleanor became ill with cancer, she worried about what would happen to her "buddies" if she died. She finally decided to have her family put them to sleep when she died.

Eleanor endured surgery, chemotherapy, radiation therapy, and even some holistic remedies, but she continued to go downhill. Eleanor's family came in to visit her at the hospital to say their last good-byes. She was so ill, she didn't even recognize them. No one thought she could last the day. Because the family was from out of state, and time short, they decided to put the pets to sleep so they would only need to take care of the funeral arrangements when she died. To everyone's surprise, Eleanor rallied. She lived two more long, lonely years. She often said she wished they had put her to sleep instead of her buddies.

Parents have a special responsibility. They need to make provision for the care of their child in the event they both die or become incapacitated before the child is grown. It is unusual for a child to lose both parents but it does happen and parents need to provide for this eventuality.

If you have a minor child, you can appoint someone in your Will to be the guardian of your child, in the event that the other parent is incapacitated or deceased. If the child's other parent makes a Will naming a different person to be the child's guardian, then the guardian appointed by the last parent to die is given priority (AZ 14-5202).

Naming a person as guardian in your Will does not impose any legal duty on that person to do the job, so before making the appointment you need to check with the proposed guardian to be sure they want to accept the responsibility. If the guardian agrees, then explain that in the event that you and the other parent die, the guardian needs to go to the court where the Will is being probated to accept the appointment. The guardian is required to give written notice of his/her acceptance to the person who is caring for the child or to the child's nearest adult relation (AZ 14-5202).

Of equal importance is to choose someone who is acceptable to the child. If the child is not compatible with the person you have chosen, then once the child is fourteen, he/she can file a written objection with the court. The court will consider the objection and may decide to appoint someone else as guardian (AZ 14-5303).

SUPPORTING THE CHILD

As any parent is well aware, it is expensive to raise a child. A guardian is not responsible to support the child. In fact, the guardian has the right to ask the court to be compensated for his/her services in caring for the child (Arizona statute 14-5209 (D)). People that you might consider to be the best choice to serve as your child's guardian might not be able to do so unless you leave sufficient monies to pay for the care of the child.

If you are a person of limited finances, then consider purchasing a term life insurance policy on your life and the life of the other parent of the child. If you can only afford one policy, then insure the life of the parent who contributes most to the support of the child. Term insurance policies are relatively inexpensive if you limit the term to just that period of time until your child becomes an adult. Some companies offer a combination of term life and disability insurance. As with any other purchase, it is important to comparison shop to obtain the best price for the coverage.

You can name the child's other parent as the beneficiary of the policy, with the child as an alternate beneficiary. If both parents die, then the court will appoint a conservator to use the insurance funds for the child's maintenance. The court will require that the conservator give the court an annual accounting to be sure that the monies are being spent for the child's support and education. Once the child turns 18, the court will supervise the distribution of whatever monies remain to the child.

 **LAWYER**   TRUST FOR CARE OF CHILD

If you have sufficient monies to care for your child until the child reaches adulthood, then consult with an attorney about drafting a Will with a trust provision in the event you die before the child is grown. You will need to appoint a trustee to handle the trust funds as the child is growing. You can appoint the other parent of the child as the trustee or anyone else you think will handle the funds responsibly. You can appoint the same person to serve as trustee as you have chosen to serve as guardian, but it may be better to appoint two different people for these jobs. The desirable qualities of a guardian are essentially that of a "people person" — someone who is sensitive to the child's emotional needs. The qualities to seek in a trustee are honesty, trustworthiness , and a knowledge of money matters.

The trustee will be in charge of giving money from the trust to the guardian for the child's maintenance. Consider choosing a trustee who is not overly generous so that all of the funds will be spent before the child is grown, yet not so thrifty that the child has little quality of life in his formative years.

If you are successful in your choices, the child will be fortunate to have two such adults to guide him through his childhood.

| Special Situation | PROVIDING FOR THE INCAPACITATED |

If you are the caretaker or legal guardian of someone who is incapacitated, then in addition to preparing your own estate plan, you need to be concerned about what will happen to the incapacitated person should you die. Someone will need to make medical decisions for the incapacitated person and see to it that he/she is properly housed and fed.

Often a family member will agree to take responsibility for the care of an incapacitated person in the event that the caretaker dies. But perhaps no one wants the job, opposite case, too many want to have control. mple, if a parent is incapacitated, one child ant the parent to remain at home with the ce of a home health care worker. Another child ink the best place for the parent is an assisted acility with 24 hour care. The caretaker spouse concerned that a tug-of-war will erupt once he n such cases, the caretaker should consult with an attorney to ensure future care for the incapacitated person. The attorney may suggest establishing a trust or putting a provision in the caretaker's Will for the appointment of a legal guardian.

Arizona statute 14-5301 authorizes a caretaker to make provision in his Will for the appointment of a guardian of the incapacitated person. Once the caretaker dies, the Will is filed in the Probate division of the Superior Court. The guardian needs to accept the appointment and give notice of his acceptance to the incapacitated person and his nearest adult relative. Once the guardianship is in place, the court will supervise the care of the incapacitated person until he/she dies.

 **LAWYER**

SPECIAL NEEDS TRUST FOR THE INCAPACITATED

For most incapacitated persons, the government and the incapacitated person's family work together to care for the person. The federal government works with the state government to provide programs such as social security disability benefits and custodial nursing home care under the Medicaid program. The family often provides for the incapacitated person's *special needs*, such as clothing, hobbies, special education, outings to a movie or special event — things that give the incapacitated person some quality of life.

To be eligible for government assistance the incapacitated person must be essentially without funds. Caretakers fear that leaving money to the incapacitated in a will or trust will disqualify him/her from further government assistance. Understanding this dilemma, the federal government allows caretakers to establish a *Special Needs* trust.

One type of Special Needs Trust is the *Disability Trust* as authorized by 42 U.S.C. 1382c(a)(3). This trust may be established by a caretaker for an incapacitated person who is under the age of 65. A trustee is appointed to use trust funds to provide for the special needs of the incapacitated. If any trust funds remain after the incapacitated dies, then they must be used to reimburse the state for monies expended by the state on behalf of the incapacitated person.

There are other types of special needs trusts that are allowed under the law. An experienced Elder Law attorney can assist the caretaker in preparing a Will or trust that will provide for the incapacitated person once the caretaker is deceased.

 **LAWYER**

WILL IS NOT BEST VEHICLE FOR A LARGE ESTATE

A simple Will is not the best route to go if you have a large estate. The cost of probate is significant for large estates. The person appointed as Personal Representative is entitled to reasonable compensation as is the attorney who represents him (AZ 14-3719).

If your estate is large and you have property in more than one state, then there will need to be multiple probate procedures. Each state will need to have an ancillary Personal Representative appointed, and each Personal Representative will need to be represented by counsel. In some states (Florida, for example) it is the practice for the Personal Representative to charge a fee that is a percentage of the estate (usually 3%). The attorney for the Personal Representative may charge another 3%. The cost of probating property in more than one state could be significant.

If your estate is large enough to incur Estate taxes (see page 34 for the table of values) then it is important to consult with an experienced Estate Planning attorney for several reasons:
   ❋ to avoid probate
   ❋ to reduce, if not eliminate, Estate taxes
   ❋ to protect your assets during your lifetime
   ❋ to preserve your assets for the next generation.

ARRANGING TO PAY BILLS

When people draft a Will they are more concerned about giving their possessions away than they are about taking into account what they actually have to give. This was the case with Larry. He had no family to speak of. After his wife died, he bought a condominium in South Florida. Over the years, he developed a close network of friends. They became his family. Larry did not have much money. His car was leased. He had a mortgage on the condominium. He wanted his friends to know how much they meant to him so he had a Will drafted giving all he owned to five close friends.

The friends appreciated the gesture but the probate procedure turned out to be a nightmare. They had to keep current the mortgage payments and the maintenance fees until the condominium was sold. Because Larry left little cash, this money had to come out of the beneficiaries' pockets. Two were living on their social security income and they had to borrow money from the others to contribute to their share of the upkeep.

The beneficiaries had no money to settle the lease on the car. Even if they did, they decided that there was no point in doing so because the amount needed to obtain clear title was greater than the current market value of the car. The beneficiaries decided not to make any further payment and they returned the car to the leasing agent.

Their decision turned out to be a losing proposition. The leasing agent took the car, sold it and then sued the estate for the balance of the monies owed on the lease.

Because the beneficiaries had to quickly liquidate the estate, the condominium sold for less than it would have had they the time, energy and resources to fix it up. After they settled with the leasing agent, paid off the funeral expenses, mortgage, and probate fees there was only a few hundred dollars left. That was a lot of work and stress for nothing.

The pity was that Larry could have arranged his finances so that his beneficiaries were not burdened by his debt. He could have taken out mortgage insurance as part of the loan package. In most cases the cost of the insurance is nominal and is included as part of the monthly mortgage payment.

Larry could have done the same when he leased the car. Most leasing contracts offer term life insurance as an option. The cost of such insurance depends on the age of the person, the term of the loan and the amount of monies owed, but the premium paid each month is just a small fraction of the loan payment.

Even if Larry just arranged for payment of one of these debts, his beneficiaries would have come away with the gift that Larry intended, instead of the headache they inherited.

PROVIDE FOR CREDIT CARD DEBT

If you have significant credit card debt, you need to consider how that debt will be paid once you die. Most credit card companies offer insurance so that should you die, any outstanding balance is paid. Lenders offer term insurance as part of the credit package because they are assured of prompt payment should the borrower die. Of course, if you have little or no assets and no one other than yourself is liable to pay the debt, you may have no incentive to pay for insurance that can only benefit the lender.

As discussed in Chapter 4, if a credit card is in two names, both parties are equally liable to pay the debt. If you hold a credit card jointly, the joint owner of that credit card will be responsible to pay for items that you purchased and vice versa. Once one of you dies, the other is responsible to pay the bill regardless of who ran up the bill. The better route is for each of you to have your own credit card.

If you are married, you may think that it doesn't make much difference whether you hold a credit card in your name only or together with your spouse because the creditor can always demand payment from your community property. But consider that if you hold the card jointly, the creditor has access to your separate property as well as your community property. Still another reason not to hold a joint credit card is that each of you can establish your own line of credit. This is especially important if one of the partners is retired or has been out of the job market for any period of time. Should the breadwinner die it may be difficult for the surviving spouse to establish credit if he/she has no recent work record It is easier for the unemployed partner to establish a line of credit when he/she is married to someone who is working.

PURCHASE INSURANCE

Rather than purchase term insurance each time you lease a car or mortgage a home, you might consider a single life insurance policy sufficient to cover all of your current debt. This strategy works best if you are married and your spouse is jointly liable for the mortgage and car payment.

If you name your spouse or child as beneficiary of your life insurance policy that is no more than $20,000 in value, and they are not legally obliged to pay your debts, then none of your creditors can force them to use any part of those funds to pay your debts (AZ 33-1126 A.1). If you want to be sure that your spouse or child receives at least $20,000 after you are gone, not reduced by the cost of probate or to pay off your debts, then this strategy should accomplish your goal.

Which brings us to the issue of life insurance — should you have it? How much is enough? The answer to these questions depends on what this author considers to be the "sleep at night" factor, namely how much insurance do you need to make you not worry about insurance coverage when you go to sleep at night? It is often more an emotional than financial issue.

Some people have an "every man for himself" attitude and are content to have no insurance at all. Others worry about how their loved ones will manage if they are not around to support them. The same person may have different thoughts about insurance coverage as the circumstances of their life changes — from no coverage in their bachelor days to more-than-enough coverage in their child rearing days to just-enough-to-bury-me in their senior years.

Insurance companies recognize that people's needs change over the years. Many companies offer flexible insurance coverage. As with any consumer item, it is a good idea to shop around. For those with a personal computer you can hook up to the Internet and use a search engine to give you a panoramic view of the current insurance market.

ANNUITIES TO SPREAD OUT BENEFITS

Most people go through their inheritance within two years. For many, the reason the money is gone so soon, is that there just wasn't much money to inherit in the first place. But for others, it's a spending spree.

People's spending habits remain much the same throughout their lifetime. Some people are born squirrels, always saving for the winter. For others, it's
Earn-A-Penny   Spend-A-Penny

Most of us fall somewhere in between. We are not extravagent in our spending habits, yet it is a struggle to save. But why should we struggle to purchase an insurance policy if the intended beneficiary will spend it all in a few months?

If you want to leave an insurance policy benefit to someone you love, but if the intended beneficiary is immature, or a born spendthrift, then a simple solution to the problem may be to purchase an annuity rather than life insurance. The annuity can be set up so that the beneficiary receives money on a monthly, or yearly basis, rather than a single lump sum payment when you die. There are many different types of annuities, so again, it is important to shop around.

CHOOSING THE RIGHT ESTATE PLAN

JOINT OWNERSHIP?
A POD ACCOUNT?
A TOD ACCOUNT?
A TRUST?
A WILL?
AN INSURANCE POLICY???

This chapter offers so many options that the reader may be more confused than when he was blissfully unenlightened.

As with most things in life, you may find there are no ultimate solutions, just alternatives. The right choice for you is the one that best accomplishes your goal. This being the case, you first need to determine what you want to accomplish with the money that you leave. Think about what will happen to your property if you were to die suddenly, without making any plan different from the one you now have.
Who will get your property?
Will they need to go through probate?
Will there be any estate tax?

If the answers to these questions are not what you wish, then you need work to re-title your property to accomplish your goals. For those with significant assets — especially if your estate will need to pay estate taxes, a trip to an experienced Estate Planning attorney may be well worth the consultation fee.

Once you are satisfied with your estate plan, then the final thing to determine is whether your heirs will be able to locate your assets once you are deceased.

Most people have their business records in one place, their Will in another place, car titles and deeds in still another place. When someone dies, their beneficiaries may feel as if they are playing a game of "hide and seek" with the decedent. The game might be fun if it were not for the fact that things not found may be forever lost. For example, suppose you die in an accident and no one knows you are insured by your credit card company for accidental death in the amount of $50,000. The only one to profit is the insurance company, which is just that much richer because no one told them that you died as a result of an accident.

How about a key to a safe deposit box located in another state? Will anyone find it? Even if they find the key, how will they find the box?

It is not difficult to arrange things so that your affairs are always in order. It amounts to being aware of what you own (and owe) and keeping a record of your possessions. A side benefit is that by doing so, you will always know where all your business records are. If you ever spent time trying to collect information to file your taxes or trying to find a lost stock or bond certificate, you will appreciate the value of organizing your records.

THE *If I Die* FILE

The first step in organizing your business records is to collect them in a single place. It can be a desk drawer or a file cabinet or a file box. Once you have all your records assembled, set up a separate file or folder for each type of investment. If you wish to keep all of your original documents in a safe deposit box, then make a copy of each document and keep the copy in the folder with a note saying where the original can be found. Some folders you might wish to set up are as follows:

📁 THE BANK & SECURITIES FOLDER

The BANK & SECURITIES FOLDER is for original certificates of deposit, stock, bonds or mutual funds. The folder should contain a copy of the contract you signed with each financial institution. The contract will show where you have funds and who you named as beneficiary or joint owner of the account. If someone owes you money and has signed a Promissory note or mortgage that identifies you as the lender, then you can store such documents in this folder as well.

If you have a safe deposit box, then keep a record of the location of the box and box number in this folder. Make a copy of all of the items in the box (including jewelry), and place the copies in a folder entitled CONTENTS OF SAFE DEPOSIT BOX. You may wish to attach an envelope to the folder and put your safe deposit key in that envelope. As explained on page 62, it may take a probate procedure to remove items from the box once you die. Consider allowing someone you trust to be able to gain entry to the box in the event of your incapacity or death.

🗀 THE DEED FOLDER

Many people save every scrap of paper associated with the closing of real property. If you recently closed on some real estate and there was a mortgage involved in the purchase, you probably walked away from closing with enough paper to wallpaper your kitchen. If you wish, you can keep all of those papers in a separate file that identifies the property, for example:
CLOSING PAPERS FOR THE PHOENIX PROPERTY

Set aside the original deed (or a copy if the original is in a safe deposit box) and place it into a separate DEED FOLDER. Include deeds to parcels of real property, cemetery deeds, condominium deeds, cooperative shares to real property, time-sharing certificates, etc. Include deeds to out of state property as well as Arizona property in the DEED FOLDER.

If you have a mortgage on your property, then put a copy of the mortgage and promissory note in a separate LIABILITY FOLDER.

🗀 THE INSURANCE/PENSION FOLDER

The INSURANCE FOLDER is for each original insurance policy that you own, be it car insurance, homeowner's insurance or a health care insurance policy. If you purchased real property, you probably received a title commitment at closing and the original title insurance policy some weeks later when you received your original deed from recording. If you cannot locate the title insurance policy, then contact the closing agent and have them send you a copy of your title policy. If you have a pension or an annuity, then include those documents in this folder as well.

THE PERSONAL PROPERTY FOLDER

MOTOR VEHICLES

Put all motor vehicle titles in Personal Property folder. This includes cars, mobile homes, boats, planes, etc. If you have a boat or plane, then identify the location of the motor vehicle. For example, if you are leasing space in an airplane hanger or in a marina, then keep a copy of the leasing agreement in this file.

JEWELRY

If you own expensive jewelry, then keep a picture of the item together with the sales receipt or written appraisal in this folder.

COLLECTOR'S ITEMS

If you own a valuable art collection, or a coin collection or any other item of significant value, then include a picture of the item in this file. Also include evidence of ownership of the item, such as a sales receipt or a certificate of authenticity, or a written appraisal of the property.

📁 THE LIABILITY FOLDER

The LIABILTY FOLDER should contain all loan documents of debts that you owe. For example, if you purchased real property and have a mortgage on that property, then put a copy of the mortgage and promissory note in this folder. If you owe money on a car, then put the promissory note and chattel mortgage on the car in the file. If you have a credit card, then put a copy of the contract you signed with the credit card company in this file.

Many people never take the time to calculate their *net worth* (what a person owns less what that person owes). By having a record of your outstanding debts, you can calculate your net worth whenever you wish.

📁 THE TAX RECORD FOLDER

Your Personal Representative (or next of kin) will need to file your final income tax return. Keep a copy of your tax returns (both federal and state) for the past three years in the TAX RECORD FOLDER.

📁 THE PERSONAL RECORD FOLDER

The PERSONAL RECORD FOLDER should include documents that relate to you personally, such as a birth certificate, naturalization papers, pre-nuptial or post- nuptial agreement, Will or Trust, marriage certificate, divorce papers, army records, social security card; etc. If you have a Health Care Directive or a Power of Attorney, then this is a good place to keep those documents.

FOR FEDERAL RETIREES

If you are a Federal Retiree, then you should have received your PERSONAL IDENTIFICATION NUMBER (PIN) and your survivor annuitant should have received his/her own PIN as well. It is relatively simple to obtain this during your lifetime, but it may be difficult and/or stressful for your survivor annuitant to work through the system once you are gone. To get information about obtaining these numbers you can call the RETIREMENT INFORMATION OFFICE at:
1-888-767-6738
for the hard of hearing, call 1-800-878-5707

Upon your death, your family may be entitled to death benefits. These benefits are not automatic. Your family member (your "survivor") must apply for them by submitting a death claim to the Office of Personnel Management. Your survivor needs to know that it is necessary to apply and also how to apply. See page 28 for an explanation about how to apply for benefits and then make that information available to your family. You can either put this information in the insurance/ pension folder or in your Personal Record folder.

GAMES DECEDENTS PLAY

We discussed the game of "hide and seek" some decedents play with their heirs. A variation of that game is the "wild goose chase." The decedent never updates his files, so his records are filled with all sorts of lapsed insurance policies, promissory notes of debts long since paid; brokerage statements of securities that have been sold. The family spends much time trying to locate the "missing" asset.

The best joke is to keep the key to a safe deposit box that you are no longer leasing. That will keep folks hunting for a long time!

If you do not have a wicked sense of humor, then do your family a favor and update your records on a regular basis. The day after you file your income tax statement each year is a good time to do so, because your tax return gives you a summary of your financial transactions for the year.

THE *If I Die* FILE

In addition to keeping your up-to-date records in a single place, you need to let your family know the location of these items. You can set up an *If I Die* file and give that file to your next of kin or the person you appointed as Personal Representative in your Will. You can use the form on the opposite page as a basis for the information to include in the file.

If I Die

then the following information will help to settle my estate:

INFORMATION FOR DEATH CERTIFICATE

MY FULL LEGAL NAME _____

MY SOCIAL SECURITY NO. _____

MY USUAL OCCUPATION _____

BIRTHDATE AND BIRTH PLACE _____

If naturalized, date & place _____

MY FATHER'S NAME _____

MY MOTHER'S MAIDEN NAME _____

PERSONS TO BE NOTIFIED OF MY DEATH

_____

_____

_____

LOCATION OF BURIAL SITE

_____

LOCATION OF PRENEED FUNERAL CONTRACT

_____

FOR VETERAN or SPOUSE BURIAL IN A NATIONAL CEMETERY:

BRANCH_____SERIAL NO._____

VETERAN'S RANK _____

VETERAN'S VA CLAIM NUMBER _____

DATE AND PLACE OF ENTRY INTO SERVICE:

_____

DATE AND PLACE OF SEPARATION FROM SERVICE:

_____

LOCATION OF OFFICIAL MILITARY DISCHARGE
    OR DD 214 FORM_____

LOCATION OF LEGAL DOCUMENTS

WILL OR TRUST _____

DEEDS _____

MORTGAGES _____

TITLE TO MOTOR VEHICLES _____

HEALTH CARE DIRECTIVES _____

NAME, PHONE NO. OF ATTORNEY _____

LOCATION OF FINANCIAL RECORDS

NSURANCE POLICIES:

NAME OF COMPANY & PHONE NO. _____

LOCATION OF POLICY _____

BENEFICIARY OF POLICY _____

PENSIONS/ANNUITIES:

IF FEDERAL RETIREE: PIN NUMBER: _____

NAME OF SURVIVOR _____

SURVIVOR PIN NUMBER _____

BANK: ACCOUNT NO._____

NAME AND ADDRESS OF FINANCIAL INSTITUTION

_____

LOCATION OF SAFE DEPOSIT BOX _____

LOCATION OF KEY TO BOX _____

NAME AND PHONE NUMBER OF BROKER

_____

NAME AND PHONE NUMBER OF ACCOUNTANT

_____

CHAPTER 9
COMPLETING THE PROCESS

The funeral is over.

Everyone went home.

You experienced and got past the initial grief.

All the affairs of the decedent have been settled.

You even did some of the things suggested in Chapters 7 and 8 so you feel that your own affairs are now in order. But is the grieving over? Do you have closure? To use a tired expression, have you been able to "get on with your life" or do you find that you are still grieving?

And how about the children in the decedent's life?
How are they taking the loss?

The death event is not over until the family finally finds peace and acceptance of the loss. This chapter deals with issues that may arise as the family goes through the grieving process.

THE GRIEVING PROCESS

Psychologists have observed that it is common for a person to go through a series of stages as part of the grieving process. There is the initial shock of the death and often disbelief and denial:

"He can't be dead. I just spoke to him today!"

It is common for a mourner to be angry — angry at the decedent for dying — angry at a family member for something he should or shouldn't have done — just plain angry.

Sometimes an ill person is aware of his impending death and becomes angry, as if mourning his own death. Relations with the family may become strained under the stress of the illness. If there was an argument with the decedent, the bereaved may be left with an unresolved conflict and feelings of guilt.

Mourners often experience guilt. Many have an uneasy feeling that the death was somehow their fault. Some regret not having spent more time with the decedent. Others feel guilty because they weren't present when the decedent died.

There is grieving even when death is long expected and even welcomed. This was the case with a wife who nursed her husband at home for nine long years. Her husband suffered from debilitating strokes, a chronic heart condition, and finally failing kidneys. She often said "Some things are worse than death." Yet when he died, she was surprised at the depth of her emotions.

Although professionals in the fields of psychiatry and psychology have observed that guilt and anger are stages of grieving, there is no agreement about the number or composition of the stages of grieving.

This is not surprising. The ways people react to death is as diverse as there are people. Some people seem not to grieve at all. Whether such people experience any stage of the grieving process may not be known even to the person himself/herself.

And there is diversity in grieving even in the same person. Each circumstance of death in one's life is different from another, so a person will grieve differently when different people in their life die. But for purposes of this discussion, we note that many people who lose someone they love report experiencing the following emotions and in the following sequence:

- ➤ initial shock, disbelief, alarm
- ➤ numbness, anger, guilt
- ➤ pining, searching for the deceased
- ➤ sadness, depression, loneliness
- ➤ recovery, acceptance of the loss, peace

COPING WITH THE LOSS

How the general population deals with the death of a loved one was investigated in 1995 by the AMERICAN ASSOCIATION OF RETIRED PERSONS ("AARP"). AARP asked National Communications Research to conduct a telephone survey of over 5,000 people aged 40 or older. Approximately one third of the respondents reported that they had experienced the loss of a close friend or family member within the past year.   Those reporting a loss were asked to describe specific coping activities that they had engaged in since the death of their loved one.

     67% reported talking with friends and family
     16%   read an article or book about how
             to cope with death
      9%   received help with legal
            or practical arrangements
      5%   attended a grief support group

When asked what strategies they found to be most helpful in coping with their loss:

     28% said talking with a friend or family
            member was most helpful
     24% said their religion was most helpful
     10% said knowing it was for the best
      6% said memories of the deceased
      4% reported staying busy as the best strategy.

It is interesting to note that 67% of the people who suffered a loss turned to family and friends to help them cope with the loss. Although talking with family and friends topped the list as the most commonly used strategy, only 28% reported this as being most helpful to them. Many times friends and family members want to help but they are at a loss as to what to say or do. The next section discusses different techniques that can be used to help with the grieving process.

HELPING THE BEREAVED

Family and friends want to help the person who is grieving, but sometimes they don't know how to do it. They may feel just as helpless in dealing with the loss as does the bereaved — not knowing what to say to console those grieving.

There are no magic words, but saying you are sorry for the loss is appropriate and generally well received. Avoid platitudes such as: "It was fate." "It was God's will." "It was for the best." Especially avoid telling the bereaved that you know how he/she feels. People who suffer a great loss do not believe that anyone can understand how they feel; and they are probably correct. It is better to tell the bereaved what you are feeling:

"I was shocked when I heard of the death."
"I am so sad for you."
"I am going to really miss him."

Knowing that you share the feeling of loss is comforting to someone who is grieving.

Listening is more important than talking to the bereaved. They may need to explore the circumstances of the death — how the person died; where and when he died, etc. They may need to express what they are feeling, whether it be grief or anger. Try not to change the subject just because you are uncomfortable with the topic or with the expression of emotion.

If the bereaved wishes to reminisce about the decedent, then join in the conversation. Talk about the decedent's good qualities and the enjoyable times that you shared.

If during the funeral period, you want to do something such as prepare food or send flowers, then consider asking the bereaved for permission to do so. The family may prefer donations to a favorite charity in place of flowers. The family may have already made dinner plans for the guests. Do not make general offers of assistance. "Let me know if you need anything" is not likely to get a response even if the bereaved does need help with something. A better, more sincere, approach is a specific offer, such as, "If you need transportation, I can drive you to the cemetery."

Your assistance during the post-funeral period is more important than during the funeral period. During the funeral the bereaved is usually surrounded by family and friends and has more than ample assistance. Any offer to help at that time may not even register because the bereaved may be numb with grief — unable to comprehend what is going on around them — unable to even recall who was present at the funeral, nonetheless who offered to assist them.

Once the funeral is over and everyone has gone home, that is the time to offer support. The bereaved needs to go through a transition period and must learn to live without the presence of their loved one. In general, the more dependent the bereaved was on the decedent, the more difficult the transition. In such case, you can be most helpful if you are able to offer assistance with those tasks of daily living that the bereaved is not accustomed to performing. For example, if the decedent was the sole driver in the family, then you might help the bereaved to learn to drive or at least help find public transportation. If the decedent handled all of the family finances, you might assist the bereaved in bill paying and balancing a checkbook. If math is not your forte, help to find a bookkeeper who can assist for a reasonable fee.

But, the best thing that family and friends can do for the bereaved is just to be there for them. As shown by the AARP survey, the specific coping activity used by the majority of the bereaved was to talk to a friend or relative. A telephone call, or a card on a special anniversary or holiday, will be appreciated. You can help most with a call or a visit. It is just that simple.

Also be patient with the bereaved. There is no set time to get through the grieving process. It may take considerable time for the mourner to be able to find some quality of life. If several months have passed and you are concerned that the bereaved is still not functioning well, or at least better, then you might consider suggesting that the bereaved seek professional counseling. Try not to be judgmental when making the suggestion. Don't say "You should be feeling better by now," but rather, "I can see that you are still having a hard time getting through this difficult period. Have you considered seeing _____"

Suggest whatever is appropriate to the mourner. For example, if the mourner is a religious person, then suggest a visit with his/her religious leader. If the mourner is a social person, then suggest a support group. If the bereaved is severely depressed then a visit to a doctor or psychiatrist may be the best recommendation.

Do not expect your recommendation to be well received. The mourner may become angry or annoyed that you even made the suggestion. It may be difficult for the mourner to accept the fact that he/she needs assistance. Some people, mostly men, think it an admission of weakness to agree that they need help. They believe they should be able to "tough it out."

Some mourners may have increased their consumption of alcohol or turned to drugs in an attempt to deal with the pain that they are experiencing. If they accept your suggestion, they may need to deal with a growing addiction in addition to the problem of overcoming the grief and they may not be willing to do that.

Elderly people might think there is a stigma associated with any kind of counseling. They may insist "There's nothing wrong with me" fearing that you think they are unbalanced or somehow mentally defective.

Some people, especially the overachiever type, refuse to seek counseling because they perceive asking for help to be a sign of failure — an admission that they failed to work out the problem themselves. It's as if they failed "Grieving 101."

But those most resistant to a suggestion of a need for counseling are mourners who use denial as a defense mechanism. They may brush off the suggestion with "No. I'm alright" or "I'm doing a lot better." If they deny that they are having trouble getting past the grief, then they do not need to deal with the problem. If they deny that they have a problem, then they don't have the problem and that solves that!

In such cases, the timeworn adage, "You can lead a horse to water, but you can't make him drink," applies. The mourner needs to take the first step himself. You cannot take it for him. All you can do is assure the mourner (and yourself) that you have confidence that he/she can, and will, work this through.

HELPING A CHILD
THROUGH THE LOSS

The first thing parents observe about their second child is how very different that child is from their first child. Parents quickly learn that each of their children is an individual, with his/her own separate response to any given situation. It is important to keep this fact in mind when trying to assist a child through the loss of a close family member or friend. Because each child is different, there is no single proper way to assist a child through a period of mourning. You can help the child most if you consider the child's background as it relates to the loss:

What is the child's relationship to the decedent?
What were the circumstances of the death?
Was it expected or was it sudden or tragic?
What is the emotional age of the child? That age may differ significantly from his/her chronological age.

As an example, consider the family of Harold and Elaine, parents of three children. Emily, the eldest child, was one of those "born old" children, wise beyond her years, sensitive and shy. Her brother John, two years her junior was the direct opposite — boisterous, immature, constantly in motion. Peter came along five years later. He was the baby of the family, a cherub, always smiling, indulged by parents and siblings.

When their paternal grandfather died, Emily was 10, John, 8 and Peter, 3. Their parents expected the death because "Gramps" had been suffering from cancer for a long time. No mention was made to the children of the serious nature of the illness, so Emily was surprised to learn of the death. She shed no tears but retreated to her room and soon became occupied with a computer game.

John and his father cried together when they were told that Gramps had died. Gramps was both kind and generous with a great sense of humor. Best of all he was never critical of John's rambunctious behavior. It seemed to John and his Dad that they lost the best friend they had.

Peter did not understand what was going on; but he reacted empathetically, patting John on the shoulder, and saying "Don't cry Johnny."

When it came time to go to the funeral Emily refused to go. Johnny got angry with Emily for something or another and pushed her down. She was not hurt, but she cried loudly and carried on. Peter started whining. The whole day was hard on their parents.

The next few months were equally difficult. John woke up with nightmares. Emily was sullen and withdrawn. No one mentioned the death except Peter who was full of questions: "Where's Gramps?"
        "Was he in that box?"
        "Where did they put the box?"
        "Why was everyone crying?"

Harold and Elaine were having their own problems dealing with the loss and they had no patience with the children. The family eventually got back to normal, but it might have been easier on all of them had the parents prepared the children for the dying process.

PREPARING FOR THE EVENT

Most deaths are expected. The majority of people who die are ill for several months before their death.   Children are not always aware of a family member's mortal illness so it comes as a shock to them when it happens.   It might have been easier on Emily and John if their parents said something like:

> Gramps is old and very ill. It happens that all living
> things, plants, animals and people, eventually die.
> No one knows for sure when someone will die, but
> it may be that because he is so old and so very sick
> that Gramps may die sometime within the year.

If either child wanted to pursue the subject then that could lead to a discussion of the funeral process:

> When someone dies in our family, all of our friends
> and family gather together to talk about how much
> we loved the person and how much we will miss
> having that person with us. Later we go to the
> gravesite where we say prayers and our last good-byes.

It is important for parents to explain the children's role in this process, but like most couples, Harold and Elaine never thought about, much less discussed, their children's participation in the funeral and burial service.   Had her parents told Emily what to expect and what was expected of her, she might not have objected to attending the funeral.

Before discussing the matter with the child, it is important that a husband and wife explore their own views on their children's participation in a funeral and burial. They may find that they have differing views on the following issues:

What factors should determine whether a child attends the wake and/or funeral:

➤ custom or convenience?

➤ the age and emotional maturity of that child?

➤ the relationship of the child to the decedent?

Should the child be allowed to decide whether he/she wishes to attend the wake and/or funeral?

Should a child be allowed (or encouraged) to touch or kiss the corpse?

Should children participate in grave site ceremonies?

Should a child be encouraged or required to visit the grave site at a later date?

There are no right or wrong answers for any of the above questions. Each family has its own set of customs and values and the answers to these questions need to conform to those customs and values. What is important is that the couple agree about what they expect of their children and then impart that expectation to their children.

The "imparting" is the difficult part. No one likes to talk about death. Parents have been told that they need to discuss sex with their children. They have been told that they need to discuss drugs with their children. These are important, life threatening, issues but it is entirely possible that a child will grow to be an adult without ever having someone close to them die. So why bring up the subject?

The reason to discuss the matter is the same reason to discuss sex with your children. The sex they see on television or hear about from their friends is a reflection of societal values but perhaps not your family values. You discuss sex to impart your family values and expectations to your children. If you wish to express to your children your views on the dying process and the afterlife (or the lack of it, if that is your belief) then it is appropriate to discuss these matters when you believe the child is sufficiently mature and ready for the discussion.

Still another reason to discuss death with the child is when someone close to them is quite aged or seriously ill. If they heard that some family member is dying, they may have concerns or questions that you can answer. Most children fear the unknown and death is an unknown to them. Of course, children are aware of the fact of death almost as soon as they can speak. It is all around them. Animated characters "die" as part of a computer game. Children's cartoon movies and television shows contain death and dying scenes. A child may have a pet that dies. Children hear about people dying almost nightly on the news.

Although children are familiar with the concept of death, they do not know how they or their family will react to the death of a loved one. If the topic is discussed prior to an impending death, the child may find it comforting to know what to expect, what behavior is expected of them, and what choices they may have regarding their attendance at a wake or funeral.

AFTER THE FUNERAL

Once the funeral is over, you need to deal with your own loss. That may be a difficult process for you so you may not even notice that your child is also grieving. This was the case with Harold and Elaine. They were not aware that Emily was having a difficult time with the loss — after all she didn't even cry when she heard of the death. Had they thought about it, they may have realized that Emily was retreating into herself as a defense mechanism for dealing with the loss. Her continued sullen attitude after the funeral was a tip off that she was having difficulty getting beyond the loss.

If her parents had encouraged Emily to talk about the problem, they would have learned that she had ambivalent feelings about her grandfather. She loved him, but she felt that he favored her brothers. Gramps always played "boy" games of catch and touch football. He never took the time to get to know Emily and she resented that. Now that he was gone, there would be no opportunity for her to have a meaningful relationship with her grandfather.

People are helped most by talking with a friend or relative about their loss. The same applies to children. Emily would have profited had she been able to explore her feelings with either of her parents. Her parents might also have profited because they may have developed a closer relationship with Emily and established a pattern of open communication.

As it was, Emily never did resolve the problem. Her parents suffered her sullenness without ever a clue as to what Emily was all about. Unfortunately, this lack of communication continued as Emily grew older and ever more a closed book.

John fared better. Harold recognized that John's nightmares were related to the loss. Harold made an effort to spend more time with the boy and not to be so critical when John acted up.

As for Peter, his parents tried to answer his questions as best as they were able. Elaine had the uneasy feeling that she was not answering them "the right way." She thought she made a mistake by saying that "Gramps is now at rest" because Peter asked if Gramps was sleeping. She thought that she might have caused Peter to confuse death and sleep.

Had Elaine investigated she could have found any number of excellent publications dealing with the subject. Many funeral homes provide families with complimentary pamphlets on how to answer children's questions about death. The local library and bookstore have any number of excellent publications designed to answer questions raised by small children.

Most religious organizations offer printed material for young people that explain death from the organization's perspective. For religious families, this is a good opportunity for the family to discuss their religious beliefs as they relate to the loss of a loved one.

INTERNET RESOURCES

Many Web sites offer free publications on how to deal with the issues of death and dying. You can use your browser to locate such sites.

Today's child is computer literate. A child may, on his own, decide to seek an E-mail buddy to work through a problem the child may be having with the death. Parents need to supervise such communication because the child may be especially vulnerable at this point in his/her life.

There are Web sites that offer organized E-mail grief support groups. One such site is GriefNet. This Web site is operated by Rivendell Resources, a nonprofit organization:

GriefNet   1- 734-761-1960
P.O. Box 3272
Ann Arbor, MI 48106-3272
              E-mail: visibility@griefnet.org

KIDSAID is a companion Web site to GriefNet. They offer peer support groups for children who are dealing with a loss. Parental permission is required before the child is allowed to join a support group.

    http://www.griefnet.org/KIDSAID/kids2kids.html

THE TROUBLED CHILD

Most deaths are from natural causes. The death is expected and not all that difficult for the family to finally accept. The *problem death* is one that is tragic, unexpected, and/or a death that cuts short a life. More and more school officials are recognizing that the loss of a member of the school community deeply affects the student population. Many schools have adopted a policy of having school psychologists counsel the children soon after the death occurs. They do not wait until a school child shows signs of being disturbed by the event.

It would be well for parents to adopt the same policy. Specifically, if your family suffers a problem death then consider seeking the services of a professional who is experienced in grief counseling just as soon after the death as is practicable.

A death does not always need to be a problem death to cause a problem in a child. As discussed before, if a child has unresolved issues, then that child may need professional assistance in coping with the loss. Children do not manifest grief or depression in the same way as adults, so look for changes that are atypical of the child and that do not resolve themselves within a reasonable time after the death. Consider consulting with a child psychologist if your child exhibits unusual or antisocial behavior such as:

> eating too much or too little

> destructive or aggressive behavior

> sleeping too much or too little

> sudden change in school performance

> misbehaving at school

The red flag, signaling an immediate need for counseling, is a child who talks or writes about committing suicide. It is important to act quickly to show the child that you understand that he/she is having a rough time and that you and the doctor are going to assist the child with the problem.

There are any number of resources in the community to assist the child, from school counselors to religious organizations. The American Psychological Association offers a referral service for psychologists throughout the state. You can reach them at (602) 675-9477.

For those who cannot afford private care, counties offer low-cost services on an ability to pay basis. Some religious organizations offer counseling services to their members, as well as to the general public, on a sliding scale basis.

Before seeking counseling services, it is important to schedule a physical checkup for the child. There is a chance that the problem is physiological. Some illnesses cause behavioral changes; for example, food allergies can cause aggressive behavior. Hearing or visual deficiencies can cause a child to withdraw into himself. Even infections can cause behavioral disturbances. Perhaps the child is on drugs and an examination should pick that up. All these things need to be ruled out prior to counseling.

If your child has been treated by the physician over the years, the doctor may know the child well enough to be able to offer some insight into the problem. If the checkup does not reveal a physical problem, the physician may be able to suggest the right type of treatment, i.e., psychologist or psychiatrist, and perhaps give you a referral.

CHOOSING THE RIGHT COUNSELOR

There was a film called GOODWILL HUNTING in which a troubled, but brilliant, teenager was required, by court order, to attend counseling. The most comical part of the film was the manner in which the boy went through counselors. He deliberately alienated (and was alienated by) several doctors until he met the right one for him. Similarly, if your child needs counseling you might need to interview several counselors before you find someone with whom your child can work; someone who speaks on his/her level — someone the child can trust.

The issue of trust may create a dilemma for the parent. The child is the counselor's patient. The counselor cannot betray the child's trust by revealing what was said during treatment, yet parents need to know whether the treatment is helping the child. The counselor can, and should, disclose to the parent the diagnosis, prognosis and type of proposed treatment. The parents need to employ someone they trust to pursue the course of treatment that they have determined is best for their child.

In seeking a counselor, personal references are the best avenue, although it may be difficult to find a friend or relation who has had his/her child successfully treated for a similar problem. With or without references, you need to investigate the counselor's background. What is his/her training? What percentage of the practice is devoted to children in this age group? Is the counselor experienced in working with children who are having difficulty coping with the loss of a loved one?

Interview more than one counselor before making your choice. If the child is sufficiently mature and able to cooperate in choosing the right counselor, then that is an important step forward. If not, you may need to be assertive and go with the counselor whom you trust and are most comfortable. If it turns out that there is no improvement within a few months, then you need to find another counselor. As with the student in GOODWILL HUNTING, it may take several tries before you come upon someone who can help your child.

STRATEGIES TO COPE WITH THE LOSS

Once the person accepts the fact of death, they are past the initial phase of the grief process. Most people do very well and are able to go through the remaining stages with no overt effort on their part. Others suffer profoundly and need to find ways to get through the grieving process. If you have recently experienced a loss and are having difficulty coping with the loss then consider your own personality type and explore those strategies that might help you through.

Do you enjoy socializing with people or do you prefer solitary activities? Are you a "do-it-yourself" type of person or do you feel more at ease with someone leading you through the process?

STRATEGIES FOR THE PRIVATE PERSON

If you find socializing to be difficult, then consider non-social activities such as reading a self help book. There are many excellent publications that explore the grieving process and how to adjust to the loss.

Praying or quiet meditation may offer you consolation. This may be a good time to explore different kinds of meditative techniques. You can find books on meditative techniques such as Zen or visualization in the Philosophy section of the library or bookstore. You can find books on Yoga in the exercise section.

If you are computer literate, then you can use your browser to locate an Internet support group. An anonymous friend may be the perfect confidant to help you to work through the sadness and loneliness that you are feeling.

INTERNET SUPPORT GROUPS

You can locate E-mail support groups for people who are dealing with all types of grief issues by searching the following topics:

GRIEF   MOURNING   DEATH   DYING

STRATEGIES FOR THE SOCIAL MINDED

If you are a social person, then consider using those types of activities that involve a social setting. If you belong to an organized religion or a civic organization, find out whether they have a support group for people who are going through a grieving process.

If your organization does not have a support group, then consider starting one yourself. It can be as simple as putting a notice in a weekly bulletin that you are holding a meeting for anyone who lost a loved one within the past year. You can hold the meeting as part of a picnic or barbecue with everyone bringing a dish for others to share. Just getting together and sharing experiences may help you and others in your organization as well.

If you do not belong to an organization, then look in the newspaper for notices of meetings of local support groups or join one of the many national support groups:

FOR WIDOWED PERSONS

THEOS   1-412-471-7779
(They Help Each Other Spiritually)
322 Boulevard of the Allies, Suite 105
Pittsburgh, PA 15222-1919

THEOS is a national organization with a volunteer network of recently widowed persons. They have support chapters in many states. If you wish to establish a support group in your county, they will help you to do so.

⛧ ⛧

AARP GRIEF AND LOSS PROGRAM
WIDOWED PERSONS SERVICE   1-202-434-2260
601 E Street NW
Washington, DC 20049

AARP currently has support groups for widowed persons in Chandler, Phoenix, Prescott, Prescott Valley, Sun City, and Tuscon. They also have support groups for adults who have suffered the loss of a family member such as a parent or sibling. Call the above number and they will refer you to the support group nearest you.

       E-mail: griefandloss@ aarp.org
                   Web site: www.aarp.org/griefandloss

FOR WIDOWED PARENTS

PARENTS WITHOUT PARTNERS   1-800-637-7974
401 N. Michigan Avenue
Chicago, IL   60611-6267

PARENTS WITHOUT PARTNERS is a national nonprofit organization for single parents. They offer group discussions and single parent activities such as picnics and hikes.

They have a chapter in Phoenix (520) 516-2079 and another in Tucson (520) 622-8120.

E-mail: pwp@sba.com
Web Site: http://parentswithoutpartners.org

PET GRIEF SUPPORT SERVICES

Those who suffer the loss of a pet may experience a sense of loss similar to the loss of a close family member. Often they hesitate to turn to friends or family members (especially if they never owned a pet) believing they just wouldn't understand.

Some local Humane Societies provide a pet loss counseling service.   The COMPANION ANIMAL ASSOCIATION OF ARIZONA provides a Pet Grief Support Service. Their Help Line telephone number is :
(602) 995-5885.

There is a list of pet grief counseling services for other states at
www.superdog.com/counsel.htm

BE GOOD TO YOU

People who suffer extreme grief tend to become extreme in everyday activities. They may forget to eat. Some find themselves eating all day. Some mourners develop sleep disturbances and go without sleep for long periods of time while others suffer the opposite extreme of wanting to sleep all day. If you find that your grief is affecting your physical well being, then you need to make a conscious effort to take care of yourself:

✶ EAT A BALANCED NUTRITIONAL DIET

Contrary to popular taste, sugar, salt, fat and chocolate do not constitute the four basic food groups. And contrary to current food faddism, no one diet fits all. The ability to digest certain foods varies from person to person and we all have ethnic preferences. You need to learn what balance of fats, protein (meat, fish, legumes) and carbohydrates (fruit, vegetables, grains) you require to maintain your optimum weight and state of well being; and then make an effort to keep that balance in your daily diet.

✶ GET SUFFICIENT REST

There is much variation in the amount of sleep required from person to person. You know how much sleep you normally require. Try to maintain your usual, pre-loss, sleep pattern. If you are finding difficulty sleeping at night, resist the urge to sleep during the day. It is easy to reverse your days and nights. Awake all night, dozing all day, will only make you feel as if you are walking around in a fog.

✴ EXERCISE EACH DAY

Exercise can be as simple as taking a brisk 20 minute walk, however the more sustained and energetic, the greater the benefit. If you are having trouble sleeping at night, try exercising during the late afternoon and eating your main meal at lunch rather than late at night.

✴ THINK POSITIVE THOUGHTS

Make an effort to concentrate on things in your life that are right, as opposed to thoughts that make you angry or sad. This may be difficult to do. During periods of high stress, you may feel as if your mind has a mind of its own. Thoughts may race through your mind even though you'd just as soon not think them. Prayer and/or meditation may help you to reestablish discipline in your thinking process.

Eating right, getting sufficient sleep, exercising and thinking positive thoughts — most people have heard these recommendations from so many sources (doctors, psychologists, writers for health magazines, etc.) that they seem to have become a cliche. But the reason that so many professionals make these suggestions is simply that they work. Doing all these things will make you feel significantly better.

But if you feel so down that you are unable to help yourself, then you may need professional help to get you through this difficult period. Check with your health care plan to see if they will cover the cost of a visit to a psychiatrist or psychologist.

ADJUSTING TO A NEW LIFE STYLE

If you lost a member of your immediate family, then in addition to going through the stages of the grieving process, you need to go through a transition period in which you learn how to live without the decedent. The child must learn to live without the guidance of a parent. Parents may need to put their parenting behind them. The spouse must learn to live without a partner, and as a single person.

In addition to learning to live with the loss, the bereaved may need to establish a new identity. Such was the case with Claire. She and Fred were married 44 years when he died after a lengthy battle with cancer. Even though Fred's death was expected, Claire had difficulty accepting the loss. At first Claire didn't think she could live without him. She would see Fred in her dreams. Sometimes she thought she saw him sitting in his favorite chair. When Fred appeared to Claire, he looked the same as when they were first married. Sometimes she thought he was speaking to her.

What was most comforting to Claire was that Fred was smiling at her. She was relieved to know that Fred was no longer in pain and was at peace. The smile on his face was a relief to her because she feared he might be angry with her for the many times he would call out her name and she would become annoyed with him. She felt guilty that she did not have more patience as a caregiver.

Claire found herself talking to Fred especially during those times that she was undecided as to what to do. As time progressed, she began to incorporate her husband's beliefs into her own so that instead of asking herself "What should I do?" it became "This is what Fred would have done."

Eventually Claire found that she was able to function on her own. She began to reengage with the world. She found new interests to pleasantly occupy her time. She learned how to live as a single person. She is now more self sufficient than at any other time in her life. She laments that Fred no longer visits her. She still misses him.

Claire was able to get beyond the grief. She did it on her own, though she will tell you that she did it with Fred's help.

Claire's case is not unusual. As verified by the AARP survey, most people adjust to the loss on their own, requiring only an assist from family and friends, but there is a percentage of the grieving population that will require assistance and may need professional grief counseling.

For those experiencing psychological problems prior to the death, the event of the death may be the precipitating factor to mental illness requiring treatment. If a person had a drinking problem or a drug addiction before the death, the event of the death may exacerbate the addiction. Some deaths are so violent or tragic, that even the sturdiest may be unable to resume their life without professional assistance. In the next section, we discuss ways of coping with the problem death.

THE PROBLEM DEATH

We described the problem death as one that is unexpected, tragic or a death that cuts short a life. Such a death is often an immediate problem in terms of the funeral, burial and estate settlement, but the more difficult problem is getting through the mourning period.

The death of a child is always a problem death. Even if the child is an adult, the parent experiences extreme grief. No one expects to outlive his or her child. In these days of a lengthening life cycle, more and more parents may come to experience such a loss. The loss may come at a time when the parent is frail or in poor health, making it all the more difficult to deal with the loss.

The only thing harder than losing an adult child is losing a young child. Nothing compares to the intensity of grief experienced by a parent when a little one dies. Some parents believe they are losing their mind. Many feel that their lives can never have meaning again. Guilt and recrimination flow, "Maybe I could have prevented it." There is even guilt for returning to ordinary living. If the parents find themselves smiling, laughing or making love they think, "How can we be doing this? How can we ever be normal again?"

The family who experiences a tragic or violent death should consider seeking professional grief counseling as soon as practicable after the death. The grief counseling can be in the format of a self-help group. Participants are able to talk and share their pain with others like themselves who understand what they are experiencing.

There are many specialized self-help groups who provide literature and peer support for families who experience a problem death.

FOR PRENATAL OR NEONATAL DEATHS

M.E.N.D. **M**ommies **E**nduring **N**eonatal **D**eath
P.O. Box 1007   1-888-695-MEND
Coppell, TX   75019

MEND has a Web site and provides monthly newsletters.

      http://www.mend.org
                          E-mail   rebekah@mend.org

☙☙☙☙☙☙☙☙☙☙☙☙☙☙☙☙☙☙☙☙☙☙☙☙☙☙☙☙☙☙☙☙☙

SHARE   1-800-821-6819
National Share Pregnancy and Infant Loss Support
St. Joseph Health Center
300 First Corporate Drive
St. Charles, MO   63012-2893

SHARE has support groups throughout the United States. You can call the national office for the telephone number of the support group in your state.

   http://www.nationalshareoffice.com
                       E-mail   share@nationalshareoffice

FOR FAMILIES OF A DECEASED CHILD

THE COMPASSIONATE FRIENDS
National Chapter: 1-630-990-0010
P.O. Box 3696, Oak Brook, IL 60522
THE COMPASSIONATE FRIENDS have local chapters with volunteers (themselves bereaved parents) to accept telephone calls.

 http://www.compassionatefriends.org
E-mail tcf_national@prodigy.com

☙ ☙

A.G.A.S.T
ALLIANCE OF GRANDPARENTS A SUPPORT IN TRAGEDY
P.O. Box 17281   1-888-774-7437
Phoenix, AZ 85011-0281
AGAST supports grandparents, who have suffered the loss of a grandchild, with informational packets, peer contact and newsletters.

 E-mail: GRANMASIDS@AOL.COM

☙ ☙

THE ARIZONA SIDS ALLIANCE
P.O. Box 1111

Phoenix, AZ 85001-1111   1-800-597-7437
 The ARIZONA SIDS ALLIANCE web set offers support group information, memorial tributes, a newsletter and workshops for professionals.

 http://www.azsids.org

FOR FAMILIES OF MURDERED CHILDREN

THE NATIONAL ORGANIZATION OF
PARENTS **O**F **M**URDERED **C**HILDREN, INC.
National Chapter 1-888-818-POMC
100 East Eighth Street, B-41
Cincinnati, OH   45202

POMC has support groups and contact people in each
of the fifty states. There are support groups located in
Glendale, Phoenix, Scottsdale and Sedona. Contact the
National Chapter for the telephone number of the group
nearest you.

http://www.pomc.com
E-mail natlpomc@aol.com

FOR FAMILIES OF SUICIDES

SA\VE   1-612-946-7998
Suicide **A**wareness\ **V**oices of Education
P.O. Box 24507
Minneapolis, MN 55424-0507

SA\VE is an national organization that seeks to prevent
suicide and to provide support groups for families who
have suffered a loss through suicide.   There are SA\VE
groups in Tempe, Yuma and Tucson.   Call the above
number for the telephone number of the group nearest
you.

http://www.save.org
E-mail save@winternet.com

BUT WHAT IF I CAN'T STOP GRIEVING?

We observed that there are five stages of grieving:
shock/disbelief,
anger/guilt
searching/pining
sadness/depression
acceptance of the loss.

There is no right way to grieve. You may pass through a stage rapidly or even skip a stage. You may get hung up in one of the stages and have difficulty getting beyond that emotion. Some psychologists refer to this as "stuckness." It's something like what happened to 45-rpm phonograph records that were popular in the 1940's and 1950's. For the benefit of the digital generation who have no experience with phonographs, the record was played by means of a needle that glided over groves of a revolving disk (the record). Sometimes the needle would get stuck in a groove and play the same sound over and over again until the annoyed listener bumped it into the next groove.

If you are stuck in one of the stages of mourning you may think the suggestions in this section to be useless in your situation because they encourage you to be proactive, i.e., to actively seek to help yourself. If you are thinking:
"I **can't** help myself. " or
"If I could help myself, I wouldn't have this problem,"
then the first thing you need to understand, and accept, is that you have no other choice but to help yourself. The pain exists within you and nowhere else. Because the pain is internal and unique to you, only you can ease that pain. This does not mean that no one can help you to deal with the pain. It just means that you need to be interactive with the healing process; and in particular, you need to take the first step.

What is that first step? To answer that question you need to identify those areas of your life with which you are having difficulty. It might help to make a list of all of the things that are bothering you. Once you compose the list, look at the last item on the list. If you are like most people, you will initially avoid thinking about what is really troubling you. It may take the last item on the list for you to admit to yourself what is really causing the problem.

Once you identify the problem, the identification itself should suggest the solution. For example, suppose you find the holidays unbearable, then a solution may be to change your holiday routine. Instead of wearing yourself out shopping for gifts, use the money to treat yourself to a boat cruise. Tell everyone that this year you are taking a holiday from the holidays. You may find that people are just as tired of exchanging gifts as you are and that they gladly welcome the change.

If your problem is being lonely, then your solution will involve companionship. How you attain that companionship will depend on your personality. If you are lonely, but not a social person, consider adopting a pet. If you are civic minded, then you may find companionship as a volunteer for community activities. If you are physically active, then perhaps you can take up a new sport or even pick up a sport that you used to enjoy at an earlier time in your life. If you enjoy sports but are not in the best shape, perhaps you can coach children's team sports.

If your problem is that you are severely depressed, then the solution will involve medical and/or psychological methods of lifting the depression. If you decide to ask for medical assistance, you need to continue to be interactive. You cannot stand passively by saying "Now heal me." Pharmaceutical hyperbole notwithstanding, there is no magic pill. An antidepressant may help you to gain control of yourself, but you still need to work through the grief.

If you feel that you have tried it all and you still are unable to find peace and contentment in your life, then you need to ask the hard question:
"What is it about mourning that I really enjoy?"
Strange question? Not really.

You may enjoy thinking of your loved one even if the thought gives you as much pain as pleasure. You may think that if you stop mourning then you truly lose the decedent. If that's the case, then compartmentalize your grief, that is, set aside a special time of the day to actively think about and/or grieve for your loved one and the rest of the day not to grieve or even think about the decedent.

Actively plan the grieving compartment of your day. You may wish to have a grieving routine, perhaps visit the grave site once a week; or quietly spend 15 minutes a day looking at pictures of the decedent or writing down your memories of the happy times you had together. If you have been discussing your grief with family or friends, restrict such talks to specific times, perhaps on the decedent's birthday, or on the anniversary of his death.

Set aside as much time each day as you believe you need to mourn, but here is the hard part — you need to exercise self restraint not to mourn, nor talk about, nor even think of the decedent during any other part of the day. If your mind wanders back to the sadness and loneliness of the loss, postpone it. Say to yourself, "Hold that thought till my next grieving compartment."

If you are speaking to someone, do not mention the decedent or how you are feeling about the loss until your scheduled grieving talk with that person. If the subject comes up during a conversation, then change the subject by saying "We'll talk about that later."

Hopefully you will find the pain of your loss to lessen over time, in frequency and/or intensity. It isn't so much that time heals; it is more that you learn to heal yourself over time.

GLOSSARY OF LEGAL TERMS

ADMINISTRATION The *administration* of a Probate Estate is the management and settlement of the decedent's affairs. There are different types of administration. See *Ancilliary Administration* and *Summary administration*

AFFIANT   An *affiant* is someone who signs an affidavit and swears that it is true in the presence of the notary public or person with authority to administer an oath.

AFFIDAVIT   An *affidavit* is written statement of fact made by someone voluntarily and under oath, in the presence of a notary public or someone who has authority to administer an oath.

ANATOMICAL GIFT   An *anatomical gift* is the donation of all or part of the body of the decedent for a specified purpose, such as transplantation or research.

ANCILLARY ADMINISTRATION An *ancillary administration* is a probate procedure that aids or assists the original (primary) probate proceeding. Ancillary administration is conducted in another state to determine the beneficiary of the decedent's property located within that state.

ANNUITANT   An *annuitant* is someone who is entitled to receive payments under an annuity contract.

ANNUITY An *annuity* is the right to receive periodic payments (monthly, quarterly) either for life or for a number of years.

ASSET An *asset* is anything owned by someone that has a value, including personal property (jewelry, paintings, securities, cash, motor vehicles, etc.) and real property (condominiums, vacant lots, acreage, residences, etc.)

BENEFICIARY A *beneficiary* is one who benefits from the acts of another person. In this book, we refer to a beneficiary as one who inherits a gift from the decedent.

BOND A *bond* as used in Probate administration is a surety bond, meaning that the surety company is insuring that the Personal Representative will faithfully perform his duties. If not, then the surety company will pay for the loss up to the value of the bond.

CHOSE IN ACTION A *chose in action* is the legal term for the right to bring an action to recover possession of personal property.

CLAIM A *claim* against the decedent's estate is a demand for payment. To be effective, the claim must be filed with the Probate court within the time limits set by law.

CODICIL A *codicil* to a Will is supplement or an addition to a Will that changes certain parts of the Will.

COLUMBARIUM A *columbarium* is a vault with niches (spaces) for urns that contain the ashes of cremated bodies.

COMMON LAW MARRIAGE A *common law marriage* is one that is entered into without a state marriage license nor any kind of official marriage ceremony. A common law marriage is created by an agreement to marry, followed by the two living together as man and wife. Most states do not recognize a common law marriage.

COMMUNITY PROPERTY Certain states (Arizona, California, Idaho, Louisiana, Nevada, New Mexico, Washington, Texas and Wisconsin) have laws stating that property acquired by husband or wife, or both, during their marriage is *community property* and is owned equally by both of them. (See separate property.)

CONSERVATOR   A *conservator* is someone appointed by the court to manage the finances of a minor or an incapacitated person.

DECEDENT   The *decedent* is the person who died.

DESCENDANT   A *descendant* is someone who descends from another, such as a child, grandchild, great-grandchild. The Laws of Intestate Succession include adopted children as a descendant of the decedent.

DEVISE   A ***devise*** is a gift of real property (land, condominium, etc.) made by means of a Will.

DISTRIBUTION   The ***distribution*** of a trust estate or of a Probate Estate is the giving to the beneficiary that part of the estate to which the beneficiary is entitled.

ESTATE   A person's ***estate*** is all of the property (both real and personal property) owned by that person.   A person's estate is also referred to as his ***taxable estate*** because all of the decedent's assets must be included when determining whether any Estate taxes are due when the person dies.   Compare to Probate Estate.

FIDUCIARY   A ***fiduciary*** is one who holds property in trust for another or one who acts for the benefit of another.

GRANTEE   the ***grantee*** (also called the party of the second part) named in a deed is the person who receives title to the property from the grantor.

GRANTOR   A ***grantor*** is someone who transfers property. The grantor, also called the party of the first part, named in a deed, is the person who is transferring the property to the new owner (the ***grantee***). The grantor of a trust is someone who creates the trust and then transfer's property into the trust. See ***settlor***.

HEALTH CARE DIRECTIVE A *Health Care Directive* is a statement made by someone (the principal) in the presence of witnesses or a written, notarized statement in which the principal gives directions about the care he/she wishes to receive. The Health Care Directive could contain a Living Will or Health Care Power of Attorney directing someone to act as the principal's Surrogate.

HEIR   An *heir* is someone who is entitled to inherit the decedent's property in the event that the decedent dies intestate (without a Will). This includes the surviving spouse and the state of Arizona, if the descendant had no surviving relatives.

HOLOGRAPHIC WILL A *holographic Will* is a Will that is hand-written and signed but not in the presence of witnesses. Some states do not recognize a Holographic Will as being valid and will not accept it into probate.

HOMESTEAD   A person's *homestead* is the dwelling and land, owned and occupied by that person as a resident of Arizona.   The definition of homestead includes condominiums, cooperatives, and mobile homes.

INTESTATE *Intestate* means not having a Will or dying without a Will. *Testate* is to have a Will or dying with a Will.

IRREVOCABLE CONTRACT An *irrevocable* contract is a contract that cannot be revoked, withdrawn, or cancelled by any of the parties to that contract.

KEY MAN INSURANCE   *Key man insurance* is an insurance policy designed to protect a company from economic loss in the event that an important employee of the company becomes disabled or dies.

LEGALESE *Legalese* is the special vocabulary used by attorneys to draft legal documents. Many consider legalese to be unnecessarily complex and incomprehensible.

LETTERS OF ADMINISTRATION *Letters of Administration* is a document, issued by the Probate court, giving the Personal Representative authority to take possession of and to administer the estate of the decedent.

LIFE ESTATE A *life estate* interest in real property is the right to possess and occupy that property for so long as the holder of the life estate lives.

LITIGATION *Litigation* is the process of carrying on a lawsuit, i.e., to sue for some right or remedy in a court of law.

LIVING WILL A *Living Will* is a written, witnessed statement, stating whether the person who signs the Living Will wishes life support systems to be applied in the event that person is terminally ill.

MEDICAID *Medicaid* is a public assistance program sponsored jointly by the federal and state government to provide medical care for people with low income.

NEXT OF KIN *Next of kin* has two meanings in law: *next of kin* can refer to a person's nearest blood relation or it can refer to those people (not necessarily blood relations) who are entitled to inherit the property of the decedent if the decedent died without a will.

PERJURY *Perjury* is lying under oath. The false statement can be made as a witness in court or by signing an Affidavit. Perjury is a criminal offense.

PERSONAL PROPERTY *Personal property* is all property owned by a person that is not real property (real estate). It includes cars, stocks, house furnishings, jewelry, etc. Personal property is sometimes called *personalty*.

PERSONAL REPRESENTATIVE   A *Personal Representative* is someone who is appointed by the Probate court to settle the decedent's estate and to distribute whatever is left to the proper beneficiary.

PER STIRPES GIFT A *per stirpes* gift is a gift which is given to a group of people such that if one of them dies before the gift is given, then that deceased person's share goes to his/her lineal descendants.

POST-NUPTIAL AGREEMENT A *post-nuptial agreement* is an agreement made by a couple after marriage to decide their respective rights in case of a dissolution or death of a spouse.

PRE-NUPTIAL AGREEMENT A *pre-nuptial agreement* (also known as an *antenuptial agreement*) is an agreement made prior to marriage whereby a couple determines how their property is to be managed during their marriage and how their property is to be divided should one die, or they later divorce.

PROBATE   *Probate* is a court procedure in which a court determines the existence of a valid Will and then supervises the distribution of the Probate Estate of the decedent.   In Arizona, probate is conducted in the Superior court.

PROBATE ESTATE The *Probate Estate* is that part of the decedent's estate that is subject to probate. It includes property that the decedent owned in his name only. It does not include property that was jointly held by the decedent and someone else. It does not include property held "in trust for" or "for the benefit of" someone.

PRO TEM *Pro tem* is an abbreviation for "pro tempore" which means "for the time being."   One who acts as a substitute on a temporary basis is said to serve pro tem.

RESIDUARY BENEFICIARY A *residuary beneficiary* is a beneficiary named in a Will who is to receive all or part of whatever is left of the Probate Estate once the specific gifts made in the Will have been distributed and once the decedent's bills, taxes and costs of probate have been paid.

RESIDUARY ESTATE A *residuary estate* is that part of a probate estate that is left after all expenses and costs of administration have been paid and specific gifts have been distributed.

SEPARATE PROPERTY In Arizona, the term *separate property* means property that is owned by a married person in his/her own right. It includes property the person owned prior to marriage, as well as gifts and inheritances received during the marriage.

SETTLOR A *settlor* is someone who furnishes property that is placed in a trust. If the settlor is also the creator of the trust, then the settlor is also referred to as the grantor.

SPENDTHRIFT TRUST A *Spendthrift Trust* is a trust created to provide monies for the living expenses of a beneficiary, and at the same time protect the monies from being taken by the creditors of the beneficiary.

STATUTE OF LIMITATION A *statute of limitation* is a federal or state law that sets maximum time periods for taking legal action. Once the time set out in the statute passes, no legal action can be taken.

SUMMARY ADMINISTRATION *Summary Administration* is a short, simple probate procedure designed to settle small estates.

REAL PROPERTY *Real property,* also known as *real estate,* is land and anything that is permanently attached to the land such as buildings and fences.

SURROGATE A *surrogate* is a substitute; someone who acts in place of another.

TENANCY IN COMMON *Tenancy in common* is a form of ownership such that each tenant owns his/her share without any claim to that share by the other tenants. Unlike a joint tenancy, there is no right of survivorship. Once a tenant in common dies, his/her share belongs to the tenant's estate and not to the remaining owners.

TESTATE *Testate* means having a Will or dying with a Will.

TITLE INSURANCE *Title Insurance* is a policy issued by a title company after searching title to the property. The policy insures the accuracy of its search against any claim of a defective title.

TRUST A *trust* is a legal document in which someone (the Grantor) appoints a trustee to manage property placed into the trust. The purpose of the trust is to benefit persons or charities named by the Grantor as beneficiaries of the trust.

TRUSTEE A *trustee* is a person, or institution, who accepts the duty of caring for property for the benefit of another.

UNDUE INFLUENCE *Undue influence* is pressure or persuasion that overpowers a person's free will so that the dominated person is not acting intelligently or voluntarily.

WAIVER A *waiver* is the intentional and voluntary giving up of a known right.

INDEX

94 LAWS ARE REFERENCED IN
When Someone Dies In Arizona

Each state has its own set of laws relating to the settlement of a person's estate. The 94 laws that are referenced in this book are very different from the laws of any other state. The author is in now in the process of "translating" *When Someone Dies . . .* for the rest of the 49 states; that is, to write a book that incorporates the laws of the state into a book that describes how to settle the affairs of a decedent in that state. The following books are scheduled for release in the year 2000:

> *When Someone Dies In Arizona*
> *When Someone Dies In California*
> *When Someone Dies In Colorado*
> *When Someone Dies In Florida*
> *When Someone Dies In Georgia*
> *When Someone Dies In Illinois*
> *When Someone Dies In Maryland*
> *When Someone Dies In Massachusetts*
> *When Someone Dies In Michigan*
> *When Someone Dies In Mississippi*
> *When Someone Dies In New Jersey*
> *When Someone Dies In New York*
> *When Someone Dies In North Carolina*
> *When Someone Dies In Ohio*
> *When Someone Dies In Pennsylvania*
> *When Someone Dies In South Carolina*
> *When Someone Dies In Texas*
> *When Someone Dies In Virginia*
> *When Someone Dies In Washington*

To order any of these books call (800) 824-0823 to check whether the book is available at this time.

BOOK ORDER

MAIL ORDER: EAGLE PUBLISHING COMPANY OF BOCA
4199 N. DIXIE HWY. #2
BOCA RATON, FL 33431
TELEPHONE ORDER (800) 824-0823 FAX ORDER: (561) 338-0423
INTERNET ORDER: www.eaglepublishing.com

SHIP TO: NAME _____

ADDRESS: _____

METHOD OF PAYMENT: CHECK ☐

☐ VISA   ☐ MASTER CARD   ☐ DISCOVER   ☐ AMER. EXP.

EXPIRATION DATE _____

PAPER BACK $20   HARD COVER $27
(Price includes shipping and handling)

	QUANTITY	AMOUNT
When Someone Dies In Alabama		
When Someone Dies In Arizona		
When Someone Dies In California		
When Someone Dies In Colorado		
When Someone Dies In Florida		
When Someone Dies In Georgia		
When Someone Dies In Illinois		
When Someone Dies In Maryland		
When Someone Dies In Massachusetts		
When Someone Dies In Michigan		
When Someone Dies In Mississippi		
When Someone Dies In New Jersey		
When Someone Dies In New York		
When Someone Dies In North Carolina		
When Someone Dies In Ohio		
When Someone Dies In Pennsylvania		
When Someone Dies In Texas		
When Someone Dies In Virginia		
When Someone Dies In Washington		
FOR A PURCHASE IN FLORIDA ADD 6% SALES TAX		
TOTAL